RIC FRANCIS & COLIN GANLEY

PENANG TRAMS, TROLLEYBUSES & RAILWAYS

MUNICIPAL TRANSPORT HISTORY 1880s–1963

Supported by

MAJLIS PERBANDARAN
PULAU PINANG
Municipal Council of Penang Island
(MPPP)

ARECA BOOKS

Published by

Areca Books
120 Armenian Street, 10200 Penang, Malaysia
Tel: (604) 262 0123 • Fax: (604) 263 3970
Email: areca@streamyx.com

Perpustakaan Negara Malaysia Cataloguing-in-Publication Data

Francis, Ric
    Penang Trams, Trolleybuses & Railways: Municipal Transport History
    1880s-1963 / Ric Francis, Colin Ganley
    Includes index
    Bibliography: p. 107
    ISBN 983-42834-0-7
    1. Transportation--Pulau Pinang--History--1880s-1963.
    I. Ganley, Colin   II. Title
    388.09595113

Credits

Book layout & editing by Khoo Salma Nasution
Cover design by Cecilia Mak
Printed by The Phoenix Press Sdn. Bhd., Penang, Malaysia

CONTENTS

LIST OF MAPS

The Penang electric tram cruising along Weld Quay, passing in front of the F.M.S. Railway Station — the latter was often called "the railway station without a rail." Passengers purchased their train tickets here and crossed by ferry to the boarding platform on the mainland.

Dedication

On behalf of the Lioness Club of Penang, I dedicate this book to the families of the dedicated workers and staff of the George Town Municipal Council who operated the public transport systems of Penang island, Malaysia.

Reg (Ric) Francis,
Lions Club International District, 201W1 Australia

FOREWORD

BY DATO' (DR) ANWAR FAZAL*

There are many special places in the world but some are truly wonderful in the way they have evolved, capturing the symbiotic essence of what is called, "soil, soul and society". The physical landscape (soil), the locus genii and spirituality (soul), and the diversity and interaction of people (society), are what make up a place.

Penang, for many of us, is one of those cherished places, with seas and hills, island and forest, and the living celebrations of all the "colours of the wind". People who settled here, from all over the world, gave life to a bustling and bio-diverse entity that began to be called the "Pearl of the Orient".

Penang's growth over the last two hundred years mirrored the joys and woes of the world, but it always evolved to meet new challenges and demands – from a trading post to a great seaport, from an instant settlement to one of the largest urban centres in Southeast Asia in the 1930s, from a town that was bombed but rose quickly after the war to achieve city status in 1957. The port grew into the main entrepôt for northern Peninsular Malaya and southern Thailand. It was a great centre for pilgrimage and knowledge networks. Penang's vitality depended on access to the world and so it made strides not only in its harbour but also had an early aerodrome now called the airport – the latter has since become an international tourist and cargo hub of some importance.

Less well known is the fact that Penang was also a leader in local transport. Believe it or not, Penang had a highly impressive people-friendly and eco-friendly local transport system, with the municipal tram and trolleybus services, the historic funicular railway, an outstanding train service, trishaw and pedal power.

We had a public transport system which any city would have been proud of. We had a municipality that provided the leadership and resources, and showed how public services could be initiated, organised and managed in the best of ways.

The story of Penang's tramways, trolleybuses and railways was a great one. As an outstanding example of people-oriented, ecologically sustainable and economically viable public transport, Penang met all the highest standards of the three "E's" that are the hallmark of good, sustainable development – equity, ecology and economics.

* Anwar Fazal is former Assistant City Secretary, City Council of George Town. He was Senior Regional Advisor, The Urban Governance Initiative of the United Nations Development Programme. He was among the founders of over a dozen national and global citizen networks, including Consumers Association of Penang (CAP) and Sustainable Transport Action Network (SUSTRAN). He is a recipient of the Right Livelihood Award, popularly known as the "Alternative Nobel Prize", and the recipient of the United Nations Environment Programme (UNEP) Global 500. The Government of Malaysia honoured him with the title of "Consumer Activist of the Year" Award in 2000.

Sadly, Penang's lead in exemplary transport was lost over time, in a frenzy of hasty modernisation and misplaced priorities. We lost a vital system, and with that, we increased our costs in human and ecology terms. We have paid a high price, directly and indirectly, through traffic jams, endless road-building and road widening, loss of greenery, worsening air quality, noise pollution and heavy petrol subsidies. As social inequities in terms of access and mobility increase, urban growth ironically translates into the decline of urban environment and community life.

Happily, we see now a stirring of interest in regaining our lost heritage. The people and authorities are beginning to take public transport more seriously. Heritage and people-friendly transport are now high on the public agenda. All this new interest and debate will be helped with the restoration of social memory and an awareness of what has been. The knowledge of past strengths and weaknesses bears important lessons for all.

The preservation of the train-tracks at the junction between Chulia Street (where I lived) and Penang Road (opposite Odeon cinema, where I used to watch films), is a credit to our Majlis Perbandaran Pulau Pinang; they must be congratulated for that. Little actions like this stimulate interest, and with interest, comes larger possibilities.

The impressive and comprehensive documentation of that glorious period of public transport in Penang, the core of which were the trams, trolleybuses and railways, will hopefully serve to restore our legacy and lead to a regeneration of public transport!

With this new classic, Ric Francis and Colin Ganley have not only done Penang and all public transport authorities a great service, they have done it brilliantly, providing details and stories of a special period of our history. Such work is rare anywhere in the world, and Penang should be proud to have this heritage documented to be read by generations to come. Hopefully, it will inspire all civic-minded people, politicians, planners, the press and the public to make Penang once again a leader in a public transport system that means good ecology and economics, a vibrant city and a community well served.

I would also like to pay a special tribute to Khoo Salma Nasution for her passion for heritage and her editorial skills in developing the final tapestry that transformed this study into another of the string of world class publications that we are becoming accustomed to receiving from her. It's people like her that are bringing forth a resurgence of interest in local history and pride.

May this book inpire more such ventures and people.

1 July 2005
Island of Penang, Malaysia

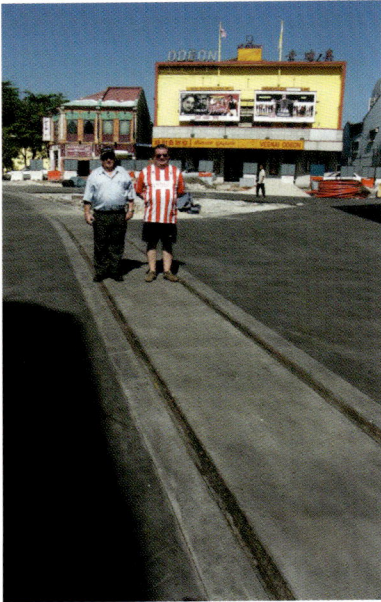

The authors Ric Francis and Colin Ganley inspecting the original tramway at Chulia Street, uncovered during recent road works.
Photograph by Khoo S.N., January 2005

ACKNOWLEDGEMENTS

Research into the history of George Town City Transport Department has been very difficult as virtually no records exist other than a few articles and references in books, and old records of the Straits Settlements Commissioners Ordinances deposited in the Singapore National Library.

Research extended from England to the United States. We would like to note a list of people who made this book possible:

This project was assisted by David W.O. Jones, of New Zealand, who executed the drawings as well as the tramways and trolleybus maps.

We are grateful to Rosy Thacker of the National Tramway Museum, Crich, Derbyshire; Michael Davis of D.T.S. Publications; F.W. York for the use of his notes and photos; as well as Ashley Bruce; the late Terry Breach; D. Watts; A. Wright; Ian Lynas and Malcolm Wade, all of the United Kingdom. Our thanks also go to John Rossman and R. Sechler of the United States.

Many of our collaborators have only been in contact by mail or email. Although we have never met or spoken to one another, we share the same goal of recording the history of tramways, trolleybuses and railways in George Town.

In Penang, Khoo Salma Nasution helped in the editing, layout, captioning and sourcing of pictures, while Yeap Ee Ban and Lim Gaik Siang assisted by scanning some of the photographs.

Ric Francis & Colin Ganley

THE TRAM

The steam tram is seen here along Weld Quay, plying the route between the Jetty and Ayer Itam, late 1890s.

STEAM & HORSE TRAMS

Penang's first recorded tramway was a steam tramway run in the 1880s by a Mr. Gardiner. Concession for operating the tramway was granted by the Government. It was more a light railway than a tramway. A Kerr-Stuart steam locomotive was used to draw two or three passenger trailers of the double-deck type used in Singapore plus two or three wagons for freight. Photographic evidence shows this to be the case with the freight wagons coupled behind the passenger cars.

The system comprised initially of a single metre-gauge line of rail from the jetty at Weld Quay to Ayer Itam Road with a branch to Waterfall Gardens being added a little later. The tramway ran, in all, about 7½ miles, of which less than 2½ miles were laid on the town roadways, the remainder being of light railway construction on land reservations at the sides of country roads or through adjoining plantations. However, the company failed to provide the rapidity and frequency of service necessary to compete successfully with cheap rickshaw transport.

Records show that Mr. Gardiner applied to run a new service from the Prison to Waterfall Gardens in 1885, to transport stone extracted by prisoners from the quarries. Permission for this extension was granted

by the Commissioners on the condition that the rails were not as such as to make the road unusable for everyone else. The Waterfall Gardens line was laid in the least populated area of the town and was mainly built so as to transport stone from Western Quarries.

Orders were placed with Kerr-Stuart, England, for three steam tram motors; these were made by Dick W.B. Brittania Engineering Works in Kilmarnock, England. The three steam trams, named 'Penang,' 'Johore' and 'Sir Hugh Lowe', were delivered between 1885 and 1887. Sir Hugh Low was the then Resident of Perak.

In the meantime, the Waterfall line was opened with a Kitson Tram Locomotive which landed at Penang, detoured from an order by Singapore Steam Tramways.

As no other names for the tram locomotives is known it is presumed that the Kitson would have been named 'Singapore'. There were eleven steam motors on these routes in 1890 and the Penang Steam Tramways Company, as it was then known, had its headquarters in Western Road just a little way up the Waterfall Gardens branch from the prison.

The business, however, failed to prosper and passed into the hands of the New Oriental Banking Corporation, which offered the line to the

A 19th century photograph of a granite quarry along Waterfall Road. The quarry was worked by convict labour. The stone was loaded onto wagons and pulled by steam tram along Western Road to the prison at Gaol Road.
Photograph by August Kaulfuss.
KITLV photograph 51561

The steam locomotives named 'Penang', 'Johore' and
'Sir Hugh Lowe' were introduced to Penang circa
1886. The locomotive pulled double-decker passenger
trailers, with freight wagons marked 'Penang
Tramways' in tow. Second class passengers sat on the
lower-deck just behind the engine, while the other
side of the same car was reserved for first class.

Bottom, postcard courtesy of Malcolm Wade

A horse-drawn tram is among a variety of transport used in Penang, circa 1901. Travellers alighting at Victoria Jetty, Weld Quay, also had a choice of horse gharries and bullock cart.
Postcard courtesy of Malcolm Wade

Municipal Commissioners in 1893. They decided against the purchase and the Tramway Company continued its career trading under the name of Kerr Stuart's Penang Steam Tramways Ltd. Herein may lie the clue to the make of most of the steam trams used in Penang – Messrs. Kerr Stuart were English manufacturers of steam tramway engines.

When the authorities considered that steam locomotives would be far too dangerous to be used in the town streets, the Company had recourse to animal traction. In 1898 the Company laid a line of light rails for horse-drawn cars. This ran from Magazine Road along Penang Road and down Chulia Street to Weld Quay. The horse trams did not supersede the others but were in simultaneous operation and, on one occasion, in collision!

> A collision between the steam-tram and the horse-tram occurred at about 5 o'clock yesterday afternoon, at the end of Chulia Street Ghaut where the Penang Road line meets that from Weld Quay... The passengers of the horse-tram were squandered about the road. Three men were injured...
>
> *Pinang Gazette,* 4 May 1899

The horse tram was not the speediest of vehicles; tardiness coupled with lack of safety lost patronage. Kerr Stuart's Penang Steam Tramways Ltd. was put up for sale by auction in May 1900 but there were no bidders.

The first electric power station at River Road (still extant January 2004). Public consumption of electricity was high at night, but during the day, excess electricity was generated and this was used to run the energy-efficient trams.

Its assets were thus bought by the Government (not the Municipality) and the whole Tramway was leased to a local syndicate represented by Robert Young M.Inst. M.E., the tramways' former engineer and manager.

In 1901 Mr. O.V. Thomas, then an officer in the Public Works Department, whose electric lighting proposals had recently been accepted by the Municipal Commissioners, suggested that the Tramway should be electrified and that the necessary current should be supplied by the Municipal generating station, then about to be established. The Government then urged that the Tramway be taken over by the Commissioners and worked electrically as a Municipal enterprise. The Commissioners approved the scheme, but changes in the membership of the Municipal Commission led to a decision not to take over the Tramway.

Early in 1903, however, Mr. J.W. Hallifax, President of the Commissioners, who had been one of the warmest supporters of the scheme, reopened the subject. As a result of an interview which the Commissioners had with the then Governor of the Straits Settlements, Sir Frank Swettenham, the Municipality was able to acquire the Tramway free of cost. For electrification of the line, the government obtained from the Federated Malay States a loan of $400,000, repayable by annual installments of $20,000 and bearing interest of four percent. The tramway finally passed to the Municipality on 1 April 1904.

An advertisement appearing in the *Pinang Gazette* on Friday 21 December 1906 was the final phase in the story of Penang's privately owned passenger tramway:

> Mr. J.W. Hallifax has been instructed by the Municipal Commissioners to sell the Steam Tramway Offices, Western Road, certain Rolling Stock, Machinery, Plant and Material formerly the property of the Penang Steam Tramways Company, comprising Steam Locomotives, Work-Shop, Engine and Boiler… A quantity of Old Wheels and Axles … and a quantity of Scrap Iron.

Penang. Last of the Steam Cars.

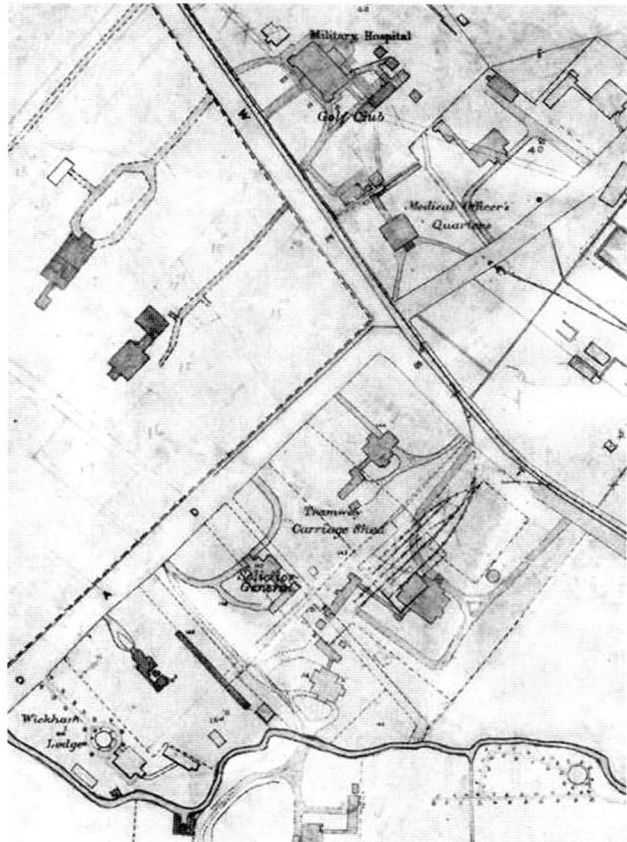

When the steam tram was abandoned, the double-decker passenger cars were left to rot outside at the Tramway Carriage Shed.

Postcard courtesy of Malcolm Wade

The 1893 survey map of George Town (modified in the early 1900s) shows the tramline and 'Tramway Carriage Shed' along Western Road at the junction with Scotland Road (now the site of Caring Society Complex).

The Military Hospital, the Solicitor-General's and Wickham Lodge are now respectively the Penang Sports Club, the Children's Library and the Penang Library Quarters.

Map courtesy of Penang Museum

Tram Car, Penang

*An electric tramcar waiting
for a passenger to hop on,
at a tram stop at the
Penang Road junction.*

ENTER THE ELECTRIC TRAM

As electricity would soon be available, the prospects of the tramway had rather improved. With the current turned on in 1904, providing power for the town, work began on relaying the tracks and constructing the electrification equipment for the trams. The overhead trolley system of transmission was adopted.

Firstly, the single track from the Jetty to the Prison was replaced by double track, and continued to Ayer Itam in single track with passing loops. This, however, was not finished until December 1905. Meanwhile Robert Young continued to maintain the service under a lease agreement with the Municipal Council.

An order was placed with Brush of Loughborough, England for 14 electric trams. These were of typical Far Eastern design – open front, toast-rack type, on a single truck frame of metre gauge.

On 21 December 1905 the intrepid Commissioners made the first journey on an electric tram in George Town. Thus George Town Municipal Tramway – G.T.M.T. – came into being.

The electric tram coming down Chulia Street.

On 1 January 1906, the regular service began on a 2½ mile double-tracked route between the Prison and the Jetty. The Waterfall Gardens branch was not converted but was abandoned; it was most likely used for storing the old steam stock until it was scrapped.

The fare decided upon was 3 cents a stage with limited first-class accommodation at 5 cents. These worked out at 2.18 cents and 3.63 cents per mile respectively. The number of passengers carried during 1906 was 1,457,357. The average receipts per passenger were 3.13 cents and average cost 2.33 cents. Up to the end of 1906 the total capital expenditure on tramways was $356,054; the running expenses were $33,952 and the receipts $45,832 leaving a balance of $11,881, or about 4 per cent on the capital outlay. As the whole length was not in full use until near the end of the year, these results would have been regarded as very satisfactory.

The municipal venture was a great success initially and the Ayer Itam route opened eight months later. This tramway was extended out through a coconut grove on a single track to the outlying village of Ayer Itam. There were 14 trams in all, operating an 11 minute service. A line was

Penang electric tram No. 8 passing in front of the General Post Office at Weld Quay.

The 'toast-rack type' tramcars, with the sign 'George Town Municipal Tramways', seen here in two photographs taken by the manufacturer Brush in the United Kingdom, prior to delivery to Penang, circa 1905.

Penang. Electrice Car & G. P. O.

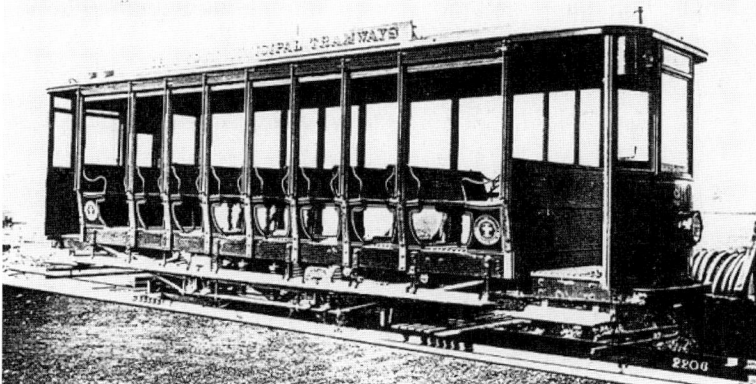

also built through densely-populated suburbs from Magazine Road to Jelutong with services from the Jetty to Jelutong also starting in late 1906.

The new depot was constructed at Tramway Road, off Dato' Kramat Road, near the Prison. The Tramway Office, located at the same site, opened on 27 October 1907 and remained in use until 1953. The Tramways were run as a sub-department of the Electricity Supply Department. The Transport Department was only made a separate entity in 1953, and this occasioned the word "Tramway" being replaced with "Transport" in the G.T.M.T. title.

Difficulties were encountered by the enterprise with declining receipts due to the economic slump in 1907-1908, and the destruction of a bridge in 1909. By 1913 the trams were making a profit and continued to do so until the trade depression of 1922. The outbreak of

Electric tram crossing the bridge at Prangin Canal.

World War I brought difficulties in the supply of replacement parts, which caused the system to run down although their gross profit reached 10.9% in 1917. At one time only eight cars were available for traffic but, despite these troubles, there was apparently no intention of replacing the trams. A period of "patching up" and "make do and mend" was embarked upon with whatever materials were available.

It is recorded that due to the poor state of the track, the section from Weld Quay to Magazine Road via Chulia Street was closed in 1921 and a temporary replacement service was provided by Thornycroft motorbuses.

Close-up of a tram stop sign lettered 'CARS STOP HERE' on one side and the equivalent in Jawi, Chinese and Tamil on the other, at the junction of Dato' Kramat Road and Perak Road.
Postcard courtesy of Macolm Wade

A maintenance tram emerging from
Gladstone Road, between Penang Road and
Magazine Road. Note the light-coloured
tram pole with dark finial and skirting.

The electric tram ran on single
track through picturesque coconut
grove in the Ayer Itam countryside.
Postcards courtesy of Malcolm Wade

All views on this page were taken around the Magazine Road Junction. The local name, 'Simpang Enam', refers to the junction of six roads – Magazine Road, Brick Kiln Road, Dato' Kramat Road, Macalister Road, Penang Road, and Gladstone Road.
Postcards courtesy of Malcolm Wade

Penang's first municipal motorbus, a Thornycroft, with a sign, 'TOWN SERVICE BEACH ST VIA PENANG ROAD' and a white board above, 'SPECIAL DIRECT TO RACES'. The bus is driving past the Supreme Court building along Light Street.
Postcard courtesy of Malcolm Wade

THE THORNYCROFT MOTORBUS

It was in 1922 that the replacement of trams with trolleybuses was first discussed as an economy measure. This came about largely because of the general condition of the track. Trolleybuses were first put into service in 1925 but the last tram was not replaced until 1936. At their maximum the trams numbered 24; a second order for seven motor cars and three trailer cars had been placed with the United Electric Car Company Ltd., and there were five miles of double track and five miles of single track.

A Thornycroft motorbus at King Edward Place.
Postcard courtesy of Malcolm Wade

The first motorbuses to be introduced to George Town as part of the municipal undertaking were four Thornycrofts which went into service in 1921. As was the case with the majority of subsequent motorbus and trolleybus purchases, they were fitted with locally-built single-decker bodywork. In this case, longitudinal seating was provided for 20 passengers. A three-quarter rear entrance was fitted with two cast iron steps into the interior (pre-war Edinburgh fashion) and the vehicles had full drop windows and a luggage rack.

In 1922 the overhead lines and track of the Municipal Tramways were in a very bad and dangerous condition. The trams were of the toast-rack type without protection from sun and rain. Derailments were so common that it was necessary to keep men standing by in the workshop for the expressed purpose of dealing with breakdowns.

The worst section of track, at the Penang Road and Chulia Street section, was henceforth abandoned and the service taken over by two of the Thornycroft petrol buses. The fleet at this time comprised 21 tramcars, 3 trailers and 4 buses.

The other two Thornycroft buses were used to open up a new service from Bagan Jermal to Weld Quay via Maxwell Road and Burmah Road. After four years use, the buses had "given of their best and were notoriously unreliable."

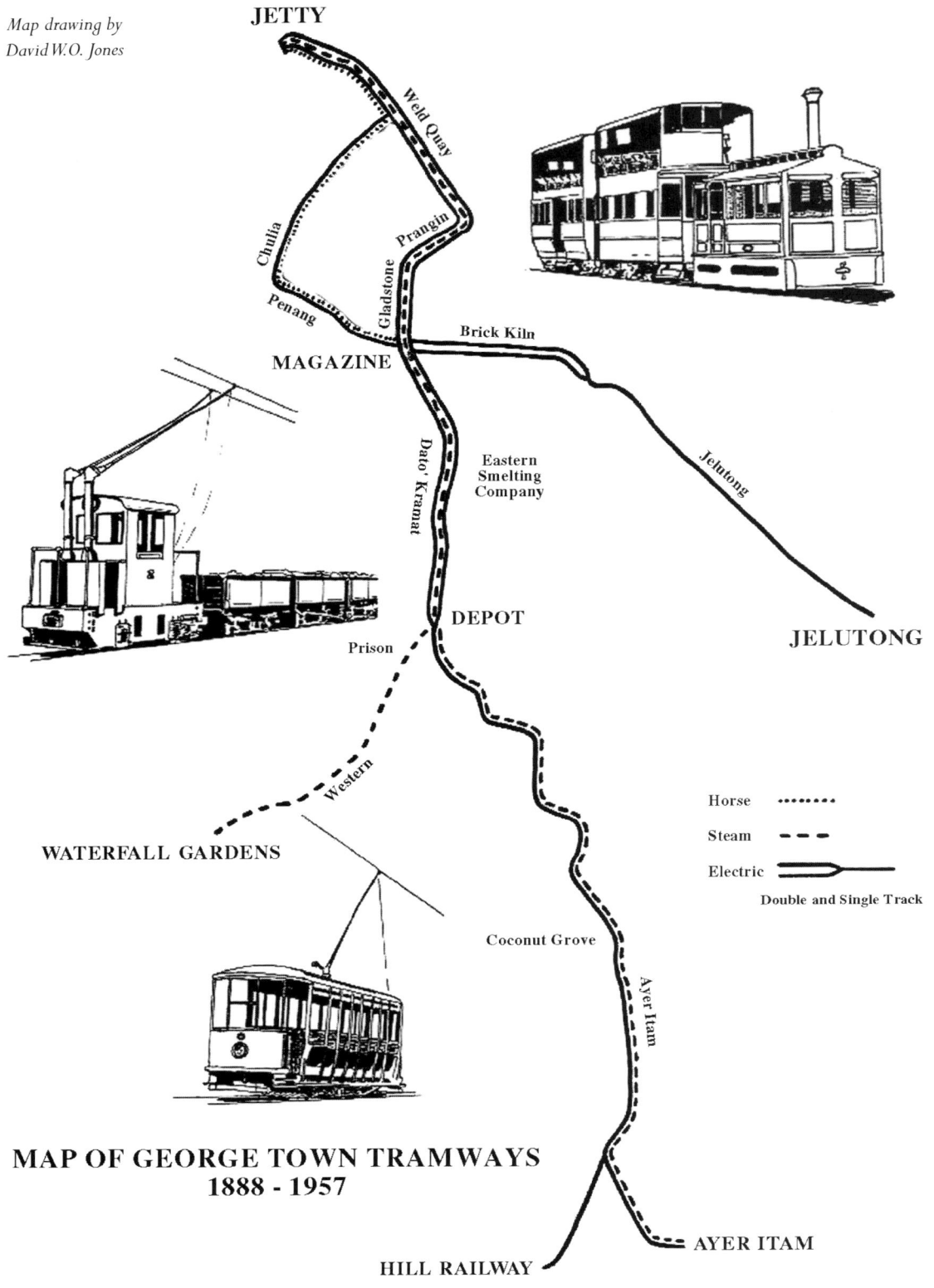

JETTY

Weld Quay

Chulia

Prangin

Gladstone

Penang

Brick Kiln

MAGAZINE

Dato' Kramat

Eastern
Smelting
Company

Jelutong

JELUTONG

DEPOT

Prison

Western

Horse ········

Steam ━ ━ ━

Electric

Double and Single Track

WATERFALL GARDENS

Coconut Grove

Ayer Itam

**MAP OF GEORGE TOWN TRAMWAYS
1888 - 1957**

AYER ITAM

HILL RAILWAY

TEIK BIN DISPENSAR

THE TROLLEYBUS

An early RSJ trolleybus coming up Penang Road on the right, passing Clough-Smith trolleybus No. 1 heading in the opposite direction.

Electric Buss, Penang.

Trolleybus No. 1 on Penang Road. Note the 'life guard', a front metal grill put on very early British-built trolleybuses to reduce the risk of injury to any unfortunate person who might happen to fall in front of it.

THE EARLY TROLLEYBUSES

It might have appeared that the trams were destined for replacement by the ever evolving motorbus, but in 1923 the Commissioners purchased one trolleybus as an experiment. Allocated fleet No.1, it was a Brush-bodied Clough-Smith, delivered as early as March 1924. Possibly the overhead was not ready, or perhaps for other reasons, the vehicle did not enter service until early 1925 and operated on the Magazine Road to Jetty via Chulia Street service.

It soon became obvious that trolleybuses – not motorbuses – were the vehicles of the future. The second trolleybus to be purchased was No. 2, a Strachans & Brown bodied Thornycroft with British Thomson Houston electrical equipment. This arrived in May 1924, the order having been influenced by the relatively successful operation of the Thornycroft petrol buses.

The first two trolleybuses could not be called "handsome vehicles", resembling as they did tramcars on rubber tyres. Two-class accommodation was provided; each class had a separate entrance. First class was behind the driver's compartment, with accommodation for six people being reached by the front door. This consisted of superior seating accommodation for those who wanted to pay extra, first class fares being about 2 cents a mile more than that charged for second class. A glass partition with a passage for the conductor divided first class from second, the latter being reached from the rear platform. Trolleybus No. 1 had accommodation for 24 second class passengers whilst trolleybus No. 2 has accommodation for 22.

Trolleybus No. 2 turning from
Chulia Street to Penang Road, past
the Leith Street Police Station.
Postcard courtesy of Malcolm Wade

Tram on the left and
trolleybus on the right, their
routes criss-crossing at
Magazine Junction.
Postcard courtesy of Malcolm Wade

Trolleybus No. 1. The body was manufactured by Brush, on a Clough-Smith chassis. It was the only one of its make.

What, meanwhile, of the tramways? As Malaya was still suffering from post-World War I recession, the year 1922 opened "in almost unrelieved gloom," resulting in fewer passengers. Something had to be done to improve the tram service, and an opportunity presented itself with the construction of the Penang Hill Railway. A new single-track branch tramline was laid from the Ayer Itam route to the Lower Station and this was completed in 1923 before the Hill Railway actually opened to the general public.

The Tramways Workshop, which employed 139 men, began to modify 13 trams in an effort to improve their popularity. However competition from private buses was now very intense. Their numbers had been steadily growing since

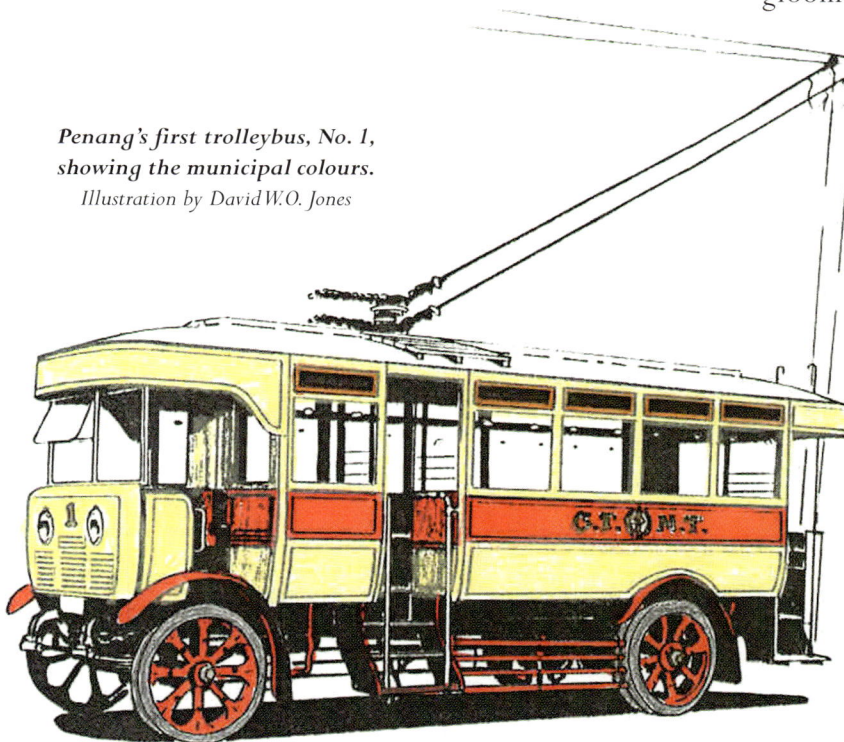

Penang's first trolleybus, No. 1, showing the municipal colours.
Illustration by David W.O. Jones

A Thornycroft Trolley Omnibus with B. T. H. Equipment
for the Malay Peninsula.

1925, and there were some 256 licensed private motorbuses by 1928.

The "two class system" must have done little to help the undertaking attract more passengers when faced with a financial crisis in 1926–1927. It could be argued that the space reserved in the trams for first class passengers would have been better utilised if given over to all passengers. The affluent Chinese preferred the rickshaws even though they were more expensive and slower than the tram, whilst the motor taxis were generally the preserve of Europeans. Most people employed in government and professional occupations regarded trams as transport for the labouring classes, so the first class compartment was never particularly well used. Moreover, the relative comfort afforded to the few first class passengers must have aroused the resentment of the many passengers consigned to the second compartment, particularly when the latter accommodation became over-crowded.

Trolleybus No. 2, the first trolleybus with tube tyres.
Illustration by David W.O. Jones

Above: 'Mosquito buses' parked along the Prangin Canal; these were Chevrolet, 1928 Model. Below: The Vehicles Office, built in 1914, at Penang Road.
Postcards courtesy of Malcolm Wade

In 1925, the Singapore Traction Company, which operated the unpopular "class system" a lot longer, found that the tram services were being drained of a large proportion of traffic by "mosquito buses". These were private buses, operating with agility over the fixed tram routes. The buses were either large motorcars or light van chassis fitted with low capacity bodies. In Singapore, legislation was obtained against them in 1930, forcing them to look to new pastures. This resulted in many of the operators transferring their "competition" to the trams and trolleybuses of George Town.

Although usually licensed for set routes in common with the trams or trolleybuses, the mosquito buses did not bother with timetables. A mosquito bus could stand at the terminus until a full load was aboard before moving off, and then cover the distance at the speed of a private car or taxi. However, for the passengers at intermediate stops, they were not so useful as the mosquitos were usually full and therefore failed to stop. Still, the "mosquitos" were a problem that the Municipality could not afford to ignore.

Ransomes'
Electric Trolley Bus
Type "C"

The general features of the above are set forth in the preceding paragraphs 3 to 15 inclusive, and illustrations of the bus and chassis are given on pages 21 and 22.

16.—The aim in the design of Type "C" chassis has been to obtain the lowest possible floor level measured from the road surface. This chassis can be fitted with a single-deck saloon body with either front or rear entrance, or both, or with a centre entrance. It can also be provided with a double-deck body, in which case the entrance would be from the rear platform. It is possible, when employing this chassis and a single-deck saloon type of body, to arrange that when loaded, the floor at the front entrance would only be 2-ft. 4-in. (711 m/m) above the road surface, and with a rear entrance the dimension would be 1-ft. 1½-in. (343 m/m). The latter dimension would apply to the rear platform of a double-deck body fitted to this chassis. In order to obtain this feature of low loading level, the motor is placed in the front of the chassis in the position occupied by the engine in a petrol-driven vehicle. This enables the frame to be swept downwards immediately behind the fore axle.

The propeller shaft in this chassis is made in two portions with a self-aligning ball bearing supporting the rear end of the front half of the shaft, the two shafts being joined together by a flexible coupling.

9628

Figure 5. REAR VIEW OF RANSOMES' ELECTRIC TROLLEY BUS CHASSIS, TYPE "C."

G.T. & M.T.

Figure 3. 35-SEATER RANSOMES' ELECTRIC TROLLEY BUS. TYPE "C," AS SUPPLIED TO THE MUNICIPALITY OF GEORGETOWN, PENANG.

Figure 4. RANSOMES' ELECTRIC TROLLEY BUS CHASSIS. TYPE "C."

MORE TROLLEYBUSES

In 1926 three new trolleybuses were ordered from Ransomes, Sims & Jefferies Ltd. of Ipswich, England. The change in chassis supply appears odd but the matter is explained in an article published in *The Tramway and Railway World* of 14 April 1927. The Municipality of George Town owned and operated eleven Ransomes battery electric-powered refuse-collecting vehicles that had given the utmost satisfaction. It was therefore a logical option to choose Ransomes trolleybuses.

In 1928, the tramways began to feel the pinch. The profits for that year dropped $2,916. The manager's response was to introduce the more popular trolleybus in place of the tram on the Jelutong route. The trolleybus service thus started working from Weld Quay to Jelutong via Chulia Street and Penang Road. With the arrival from Ransomes, Sims & Jefferies of the three complete new trolleybuses (Nos. 3, 4 and 5) this gave the undertaking 21 tramcars, 3 trailers, 5 trolleybuses and 4 antique and obsolete motorbuses, to compete with well over 100 mosquito buses.

The new trolleybuses were of Ransomes Type C, having the driving motor in a forward position in order to obtain the very lowest loading line. In other respects the chassis was similar to the Ransomes Type D2. The body was of a type

Take away the trishaw and this could be a picture of a street in London. But this is actually a scene from turn-of-the-20th-century George Town. The imposing building on the left is the Chartered Bank, which played an important role as financiers in Penang and, later, in all of British Malaya. Established first in Singapore, the bank's arrival in Penang in the middle of the 19th century signaled the development of the financial service sector in Penang, facilitating the capital requirements of European businessmen who, in turn, started opening up the country.

Reproduced from The STAR, 9 July 2001, the photo shows an RSJ Type C trolleybus and a rickshaw along Downing Street, Penang.

suitable for use in Penang's climate and was provided with wooden slatted seats in place of upholstered seats similar to those in the trams. The whole framework was built of teak and the body had seating for 35 passengers. In addition, the windows dropped down for maximum comfort and sunblinds were fitted to each window.

Survival meant expansion and in March 1929 five more complete Type C trolleybuses arrived from Ransomes, Sims & Jefferies; these became Nos. 6 to 10 and allowed for the conversion of the Bagan Jermal route to trolleybus operation.

RSJ Type C trolleybus No. 5 in front of the Hongkong & Shanghai Bank, Downing Street. Ford Model 'A' taxis are parked down the middle of the road behind the policeman's shelter.
Postcard courtesy of Malcolm Wade

The four Thornycroft motorbuses were withdrawn for scrap but not initially disposed of and broken up. This was to be the end of proper motorbus operation until the 1950s. The Municipality then operated no motor vehicle of any type until after World War II.

One Thornycroft motorbus was taken off the scrap road and rebuilt into trolleybus No. 11 in December 1929. With sufficient trolleybuses for current operations it was decided to rebuild the remaining

RSJ Type C trolleybus No. 9 showing
the original rear entrance.
Courtesy of F. W. York

RSJ Type C trolleybus No. 10,
imported together with Nos. 6 to 9.
Colin Ganley collection

tramcars to the more conventional enclosed type which were, nevertheless, open at both ends. It is said that the resulting saloons were well up to the standards of the day but this did not check the inroads into revenue by the mosquito buses.

After having all the trams modified to make travel more comfortable the Commissioners' concern was the worsening conditions prevailing in 1930. They explained where the difficulty lay:

> Competition from hired buses was again very severe, and the rules governing the control of these buses having been relaxed during the year, they were able to run as, when and where they pleased. The practice adopted by them of waiting at our regular stopping places and collecting passengers and then moving off just as our trolleybuses arrived caused considerable loss both of passengers and revenue and is hoped that some rules will be made preventing this deliberate poaching and unfair competition.

A mention of George Town's trolleybuses was made in *The Electric Trolleybus* by R. A. Bishop, published in 1931, under the heading 'The Straits Settlements':

Some time ago Messrs. Ransomes shipped a fleet of trolleybuses for service in Penang, to replace the tramway services, which were due for renewal, as when dealing with the question of an alternative form of transport to the tramways the trolleybus was again considered the most suitable vehicle.

The route mileage operated in Penang is approximately 8 miles, the roads are exceptionally good, and operating conditions almost perfect.

THE LAST TRAMS & THE TROLLEYBUS EXPANSION

By 1931, the trams were in a worse position with an actual loss of $3,101 for the year. In 1932 the loss had increased to $5,725 and in 1933 to $17,085. There were fewer passengers due to the Depression, and private buses were running on no regular schedule. The results were a new series of bye-laws introduced at the end of the year restricting the number of buses on a given route.

The legislation banned the popular Ford Model 'T' taxis altogether but the number of mosquito buses remaining was still high. In order to protect Municipal interests in street transport it was decided that the

trams should be scrapped and replaced by an expanded trolleybus fleet. This led to a large accumulation of trolleybuses by 1936.

Orders were then placed in England for more trolleybuses with Ransomes, Sims & Jefferies. Already, in November 1931, a further derelict Thornycroft motorbus had been refurbished as trolleybus No. 12.

The further Ransomes, Sims & Jefferies vehicles were all of the standardised RSJ "Small Light Type", fitted with locally-built single deck bodies. Nos. 13 and 14 arrived in May 1935 and were followed by Nos. 15 and 16 in February 1936. A report for the undertaking in 1935 stated the following:

The RSJ "Small Light Type", fitted with locally-built single deck body.
Illustration by David W.O. Jones

36

RSJ 'Small Light Type' No. 27 swinging past the Anti-War Memorial en route from Ayer Itam to the Jetty in the early 1950s. Note the green colour code of the square attachment mounted over the destination box.

One of the 1935 RSJ "Small Light Type" seen when new. The body was constructed by the Tramways Department of the George Town Municipality.

GEORGETOWN MUNICIPAL TRAMWAYS

Complete Change-Over in 31st year

In his report for the year 1935 Mr. T. Rogers municipal electrical engineer and tramways manager at Georgetown, Penang, Straits Settlements, mentions that the report of the electrical department covers the 31st year of working, while the tramways completed the 30th year of operation. Since 1928 all the tramway sections but one have been converted to trolleybuses and petrol buses, some of the latter giving place to trolleybuses, which are described as being more comfortable as well as more economical to operate. The only section left of the old tramways, which was relaid since 1904, is now being changed to trolleybuses.

Extensive experiments have been made with a view to converting all the buses to rheostatic braking. The report says "This form of braking is very effective, and greatly reduces the wear and tear on the mechanical brakes. Little effort on the part of the driver is required to operate this brake, which is purely electrical." In order to warn motorists behind a bus that the vehicle is about to stop, an illuminated red sign having the word "Brake" is fitted. This sign is illuminated when the driver releases his power controller.

A RSJ "Small Light Type" trolleybus cruising past the HSBC Bank along Downing Street.
Postcard courtesy of Malcolm Wade

The largest single order for trolleybuses resulted in the arrival of 14 Ransomes "Small Light Type" vehicles, Nos. 17 to 30 in November 1936. The stage was set for the final passenger run by a tram in George Town. This passed without ceremony on 10 September 1936 when trolleybuses took over the Ayer Itam route. It is thought that trams might have maintained the Hill Railway shuttle service until trolleybuses took over that service in 1937. It would, however, be a further two decades before the sounds of electric tramways were to be silenced forever. This situation will be fully referred to later in the section on the Electric Railway.

The process of replacing trams with trolleybuses on the Ayer Itam route had actually taken longer than originally envisaged. A vote of $200,000 was put in to introduce the trolleybuses and the change over was completed in 1937 with the use of two very small trolleybuses.

Opposite page: The largest single order for trolleybuses, No. 17 to No. 30, lined up at the old tramway depot at Tramway Road. The shipment arrived in November 1936.
Courtesy of Ashley Bruce

Special edition Trolleybus No. 1A
– possibly the smallest of its kind in the world –
servicing the Penang Hill route, seen here at
the Anti-War Memorial terminal.

THE SMALLEST SERVICE TROLLEYBUSES IN THE WORLD

Trolleybuses Nos. 1A and 2A had been ordered in 1934 and specifically built for the shuttle service from the Lower Station on the Hill Railway to Ayer Itam main road – approximately one mile. These nine-seater trolleybuses were probably the smallest service trolleybuses in the world.

They were about the size of a large private car, and looked as though the weight of the trolleypoles would unbalance them. There is no record of what they were used for prior to taking up duties on the Hill Railway shuttle service. It is probable that they were built on Morris 30 cwt chassis with parts previously used by Ransomes battery electric-powered rubbish trucks. They were most certainly "home-made". The rear was open above the waistline, and below, the body panels consisted of two doors through which could be put the passengers' more bulky luggage or items of freight.

In accordance with a decision made by the Municipal Commissioners in October 1937 to reduce the number

The "home-made" 9-seater trolleybus.
Illustration by David W.O. Jones

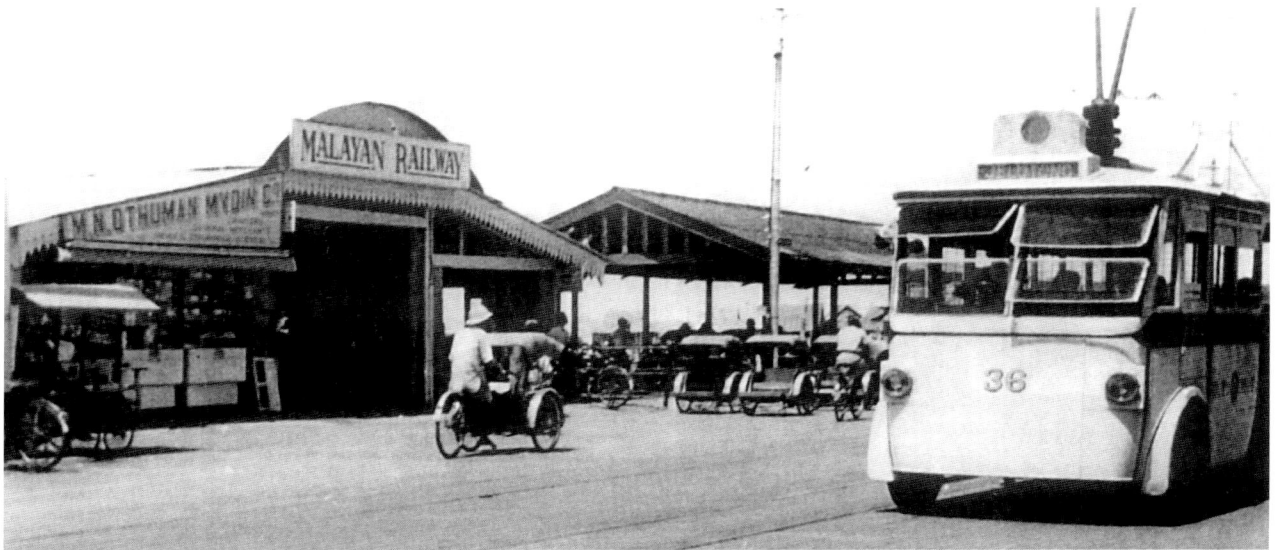

of hire buses by 50 over a period of 18 months, 17 were eliminated in January and another 17 in July. The total number was reduced from 162 to 128, distributed thus over the following routes:

Prangin to Ayer Itam	(Green Buses)	11
Prangin to Telok Bahang	(Blue Buses)	39
Prangin to Balik Pulau	(Yellow Buses)	78

The restriction in the number of licences issued was later relaxed somewhat. In 1934 there had been 150 privately-owned buses and the trams then showed a profit of $8,914. Competition, nevertheless, had had its effect, for the decision to scrap the remaining trams in 1935 had largely been based on problems with private operators.

During the year 1938, the entire system of overhead wires was replaced. In June that year, another two Ransomes "Small Light Type" trolleybuses Nos. 31 and 32 arrived, followed by Nos. 33 and 34 in January 1939. By then the 36 trolleybuses were showing a net profit of $51,557. Trolleybuses were in use everywhere, the three main routes being to Ayer Itam, Jelutong and Bagan Jermal. With a net profit of $50,070 in 1939 and $70,771 in 1940, the Transport Department had passed its difficult period and was well able to pay its way. April 1940 saw the arrival of Nos. 35 and 36, the last trolleybuses to be brought in until after World War II. The fleet strength was now 38 and a further three Ransomes "Small Light Type" were ordered for delivery in 1941 but due to hostilities they were diverted to Trinidad.

WORLD WAR II

As the tide of war drew nearer, the one hundred per cent trolleybus fleet proved to be an advantage to the Municipality, as operators with motorbuses suffered the effects of requisition by the defence forces. Initially, the Second World War was expected to have as little impact on George Town as the First World War. Instead, with the Japanese invasion of Malaya and Singapore, considerable destruction overtook the transport systems. Bombing and street fighting wrought havoc on the overhead lines and traction poles. Meanwhile, Japanese bombs devastated trolleybuses Nos. 16 and 35. The latter was very new and though the body was totally destroyed, the chassis fortunately survived and was stored at the depot. The Japanese administration did little in the way of maintaining public transport services. The lack of replacement parts, coupled with the use of such materials as coconut oil for lubricant, meant that the service was literally run into the ground.

James Tait, an electrician with the Municipal Electricity and Transport Departments, recounted a tragic episode during the outbreak of war in December 1941. When a trolleybus (probably No. 16) broke down in Acheen Street, the department immediately dispatched a rescue team consisting of senior mechanic Lim and workers Anthony, Poh Tin, 'Busu' and 'Bachi'. They arrived on the scene with a tower wagon (possibly an Austin) equipped with a wooden tower and hydraulic lift. It was a vehicle used to rescue breakdowns, one which Tait used often enough to repair overhead traction lines at night.

The bus in question was stranded in front of some shophouses along Acheen Street, diagonally opposite the mosque, and near the junction with Armenian Street (along the site of the present municipal park). While the workers were still in Acheen Street, a bomb hit the shophouses and the trolleybus nearby caught fire. The four council workers perished and

A trolleybus built for George Town service was not delivered in 1942 because of World War II; instead it ended up in the West Indies as No. 15 of the Trinidad bus fleet.
Courtesy of Ashley Bruce

A rare photograph — municipal worker James Aeria inspecting the charred remains of the trolleybus that burnt on Acheen Street as a result of Japanese bombing at the outbreak of World War II.

Photograph by James Tait

their charred remains were found in the back of the burnt-out bus. Their leader, Lim, saved himself by ducking in a ditch at the junction of Carnarvon Street, though his bottom was grazed by a piece of shrapnel.

When Penang emerged from three years of Japanese Occupation, there was not a single serviceable trolleybus. Things could have been worse as, given the relative youth of some of the vehicles, the George Town trolleybuses could have been sent for service in Japan — this was indeed what happened to the vehicles in occupied Rangoon. Singapore Traction Company, incidentally, also escaped this fate, but this was possibly because their open cab AEC 603T type vehicles dating from 1926 were regarded as little more than mobile scrap heaps! In Penang, work was put in hand as early as possible to restore services but it was a protracted task.

By 1946, the War Department found itself with hundreds of surplus military vehicles, mostly 3 tonners, and rather than ship these back to England for disposal, they decided to sell them locally. The chassis-starved bus operators snapped them up quickly, and then mounted locally-built bodies on them. In this way, the George Town Council was able to obtain

sixteen Dodge truck chassis. A crude type of bus body was built, with no attempt at comfort, but simply to provide an interim service while the trolleybuses were being restored.

The resulting motor buses were extremely hard on petrol consumption with the result that they were not kept on the road any longer than was absolutely essential. By the end of 1946, as many as 14 trolleybuses were back on the road, seven more a year later, a further nine in 1948 and the whole fleet by 1950, with the exception of the written-off No. 16 and No. 35. The Dodge buses were taken off the road and disposed of. What a truly remarkable tribute to the operator's workforce!

Post-war Malaya was overshadowed by another blight. Terrorists played one of their new tricks, bus burning, on a trolleybus at Jelutong. An eyewitness stated that it was one of the 1936 Ransomes vehicles, and it would seem that it was No. 30 that was cremated. It is also believed that arson was tried on a number of other occasions but without success.

On the plus side, No. 35 was fitted with a new body seating 26 in 1951 and returned to service.

Post-war postcard showing RSJ trolleybus No. 36, the last trolleybus to be bought before World War II, turning at the Anti-War Memorial whilst working the Hill Railway shuttle service. This must be one of the few remaining Japanese-made jinrickshaws in George Town at the time, as there were only 19 left in 1946 and no new licenses were issued after 1953.

The first postwar vehicles were three Sunbeam F4s with locally-built 24 seat bodies which were delivered in February 1953. The first, No.1, is being inspected by the police before entering service. During the Emergency, the municipal depot was a prohibited area under tight security.

Photographs by James Tait

Sunbeam F4 trolleybus No. 11, replacing an old Thornycroft of the same number.
Courtesy of Robert Sechler

No.16, which replaced WWII casualty of the same number, is seen turning from Beach Street to Light Street, on the city end of the Bagan Jermal route.
Courtesy of F.W. York

POST-WAR RECOVERY
& NEW TROLLEYBUSES

The transport system had been further extended and improved. It took several years to restore it to its pre-war peak, with only 7,181,936 passengers being carried in 1948 as compared with 14,644,255 in 1940. Progress thereafter was rapid with 35 trolleybuses operating in 1949 and the daily services extended to 10 pm in 1951. It was eventually extended to midnight in 1961.

By 1950 the management was able to look to the future and consideration was given to replacing some of the older fleet, Nos. 1 to 12. With this in mind, George Town ordered three experimental chassis from the Sunbeam trolleybus Company in Wolverhampton, England. These trolleybuses, Sunbeam F4s, were fitted with a local body with 24 seats and entered service in February 1953 as Nos. 1, 16 and 11. The original No. 1 had now been withdrawn. No. 16 was a vacant number following World War II casualties and No. 11 had been carried by a Thornycroft that started life in 1921 as a motorbus, but was now withdrawn. The three chassis had consecutive numbers Sunbeam 50742 (1), 50743 (16) and 50744 (11).

A second type of Sunbeam chassis arrived in 1954, the MF2B. This differed from the F4 as it was longer and had set back front wheels. Indeed,

Sunbeam MF2B No. 12, a publicity photo taken just prior to entering service.

Sunbeam No. 52 stopping at Weld Quay and Sunbeam No. 54, stopping at Penang Road. Both entered service in 1954.
Courtesy of F. W. York and Colin Ganley collection

in England, Bournemouth and Kingston-Upon-Hull Corporations later used this type of chassis, about the most modern on the market, for dual entrance double-deckers with two staircases. A rear entrance and front exit were provided on Bournemouth vehicles whilst a front entrance and centre exit were provided on those with Kingston-Upon-Hull Corporation.

The first, No.12, entered service in September 1954, taking the number from a withdrawn veteran. Then No. 2 entered service in October 1954, using a fleet number from another withdrawn vehicle. In contrast, Nos. 51 to 55, which entered service in October and November 1954, carried completely new previously unallocated fleet numbers. All seven were effectively ordered *en bloc* as the chassis numbers were consecutive,

To mark the Coronation of Queen Elizabeth II in 1953 a brand new Sunbeam F4 trolleybus was appropriately decorated.

48

being Sunbeam 80069 to 80075. All the Sunbeams had locally-built centre entrance 41-seat bodies of quite modern appearance.

When consideration for replacements was being made, it was found that Nos. 3 to 10 still had sound chassis, so they were rebodied in 1954–1955 with a similar style to that of the Sunbeam F4s. Externally, they could be identified by the Ransomes co-axial trolley poles.

A variety of trolley-pole mountings could at one time be observed. Nos. 1A and 2A had poles mounted behind each other, the Ransomes, Sims & Jefferies were fitted with co-axial trolley bases — mounted vertically over each other — while the Sunbeams were fitted with modern parallel trolley bases.

More SUNBEAM Trolleybuses for PENANG

The Municipality of Georgetown, Penang, has operated trolleybuses for many years with conspicuous success and like many operators of long experience, they are steadily replacing their older vehicles with modern Sunbeam chassis. A recent order for a number of MF2B type chassis is the third order placed with the Sunbeam Company by this Municipality in the past four years. The bodies are designed and built in Georgetown.

THE SUNBEAM TROLLEYBUS COMPANY LIMITED

Associated with GUY MOTORS LIMITED
Fallings Park, Wolverhampton

The Sunbeam trolleybus with a MF2B chassis and locally-built centre entrance 41-seat bodies.
Illustration by David W.O. Jones

After withdrawal from service the remains of the pre-war RSJ Light Types were still to be seen at the depot some years later. They were no doubt used as a supply of any useful spare parts to keep the later fleet on the road.

The overhead tower wagon, seen here in the garage, was an important vehicle for repairing the overhead wiring around the system. On the right was the early diesel pump at the bus depot at Lorong Kulit.

Photographs this page by James Tait

DESTINATIONS & TICKETS

Visitors to George Town would have been pleased to find that, as published in the *Penang Information Guide*, 1951,

> George Town is well served in the matter of transport. Municipal trolley and motorbuses run along well mapped out routes; the fare is ten cents per passenger from any one point to destination or terminus. The starting point of the routes is Victoria Pier in Weld Quay and from there the visitor can go by bus to places such as Pulau Tikus and Bagan Jermal. Ayer Itam and the foot of Penang Hill, and Sungei Pinang and Jelutong. Supplementary to these routes, Municipal motorbuses run between Jelutong and Gottlieb Road and Pulau Tikus.
>
> In addition to the Municipal transport buses privately owned motorbuses operate regular services beyond Municipal limits. The starting point is in Prangin Road, off Penang Road and from there one may travel to villages such as Bagan Jermal, Tanjong Tokong, Tanjong Bungah, Batu Ferringhi, Telok Bahang along the north east coast, westwards to Ayer Itam and soutwards to Jelutong, Bayan Lepas, Sungei Dua, Relau and Balik Pulau.

Visitors might have found two unusual features of the trolleybuses noteworthy. Firstly, being exempt from road tax, the trolleybuses did not have registration plates — as was the case in Singapore and elsewhere. Secondly, each route was colour coded in addition to featuring the usual destination blinds. In the case of the trolleybuses, the colour coding was in the form of a square attachment mounted over the destination box, or in the case of the ex-London vehicles a colour indication in their former route number box. The motorbus blinds were white letters on a coloured background. This provided a quick and easy route identification, especially for those who could not read English. The blinds fitted to the trolleybuses carried only a one-line display in English showing the ultimate destination, for example, "JETTY", "JELUTONG", "AYER ITAM" or "BAGAN JERMAL". Incidentally, until 1963 at least, postwar buses of the Singapore Traction Company also only had English name and number displays.

GEORGE TOWN TROLLEYBUS ROUTES
showing years of operation

JETTY – Weld Quay – Chulia Street – Penang Road – MAGAZINE
(1924 to 1928)

JETTY – Weld Quay – Chulia Street – Penang Road – Magazine – Brick Kiln Road – Jelutong Road – JELUTONG
(1928 to 1961)

POST OFFICE – Light Street – Pitt Street – Carnarvon Street – Maxwell Road (Outbound) or Prangin Road (Inbound) – Burmah Road – College Lane – Kelawei Road – BAGAN JERMAL
(1929 to 1959)

JETTY – Weld Quay – Acheen Street – Carnarvon Street – Gladstone Road – Magazine – Dato Kramat Road – Ayer Itam Road – Memorial – AYER ITAM VILLAGE
(1936 to 1960)

MEMORIAL (Ayer Itam Road) – HILL RAILWAY
(1937 to 1960)

JETTY – Weld Quay – Chulia Street – Penang Road – Magazine – Dato Kramat Road – Perak Road – Caunter Hall Road – Trengganu Road – Free School Road – GREEN LANE
(1953 to 1960)

MAGAZINE – Macalister Road – Western Road – Waterfall Road – BOTANICAL GARDENS
(1954 to 1959)

Tickets used on GTMT Trolleybuses. The serial letter/number code was printed at the top above the title "Municipal Transport Service". The names of the route termini were printed lengthwise, whilst in the central space the amount of the fare was stated – 10 cents, or in the case of half fare for children. At the foot of the ticket appeared the name 'Penang' instead of the Municipal name George Town, above the small print 'Issued Subject to Transport Bye-Laws.' Right at the bottom was the printer's name.
Courtesy of F. W. York

A 15 cent ticket improvised by stamping a 10 cents ticket with a cancellation titled 'Municipal Transport Services 15 cents.'
Courtesy of F. W. York

The appearance of the tickets reflected the colour code of the route system – the yellow route, Jelutong, having all yellow tickets, the red route, Bagan Jermal, having all red tickets and so on.

Until 1947 a system of fare tables was in operation, and whilst this was a very fair system to both the traveller and the operator, a vast percentage of monies was not reaching the management. Two reasons for this were apparent. Firstly there was a reluctance by the passenger to pay the full fare for the journey travelled, partly due to the resentment of paying the government what they saw as more in the way of taxes, and secondly, partly as a throwback to the lax and corrupt ways of the Japanese administration. Conducting staff were also diverting takings into their own pockets and misappropriation of revenue was also a major headache for the Singapore Traction Company at the time.

From 1947 up till the early 1950s, a flat rate of 10 cents (about 1 pence in current English money) applied – a bargain for a ride from Weld Quay to Ayer Itam, a distance of nearly seven miles. The flat fare improved revenue and reconciled the passenger but it did not totally solve the problem of conductors "lining their pockets."

Map drawing by
David W.O. Jones

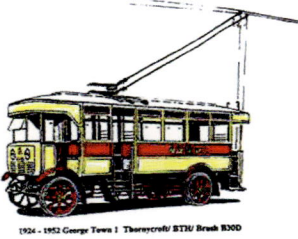

JETTY
(1924)

Esplanade
King Edward
Weld
Downing
Pitt
Acheen
Prangin
Chulia
Gladstone
Penang

1924 - 1952 George Town 1 Thornycroft/ BTH/ Brush B30D

1924 - 1952 George Town 2 Thornycroft/ BTH/ Strachan & Brown B28D

1925 - 1961 George Town 3 - 10 Ransomes S & J/ RSJ/ GTMT B26R
1929 - 1953 George Town 11, 12 Thornycroft / / GTMT B26C

MAGAZINE
(1924)

Eastern
Smelting
Works

Jelutong

1956 - 1959 George Town 20 - 23 AEC 664T/ EE/ MCCW H70R ex LPTB
1956 - 1959 George Town 24 AEC 664T/ EE/ Weymann H70R ex LPTB

Burmah
Macalister
Dato' Kramat

Perak
Lorong Kulit
DEPOT
Tramway

Caunter Hall
Free School

Perak

JELUTONG
(1928)

BAGAN JERMAL
(1929)

College
Western
Green

GREEN LANE
(1953)

Waterfall

BOTANICAL GARDENS
(1954)

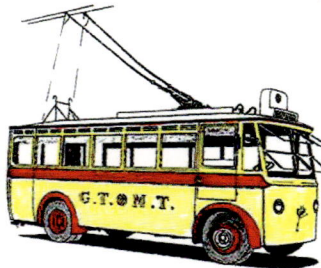

G.T.M.T.

1935 - 1961 George Town 13 - 36 Ransomes S & J/ RSJ/ GTMT B26C & R

Ayer Itam

1953 - 1961 George Town 1, 11, 16 Sunbeam F4/ BTH/ GTMT B24C

AYER ITAM ROAD
MEMORIAL

Paya Terubong

Penang Hill Railway
Balik Pulau

HILL RAILWAY
(1937)

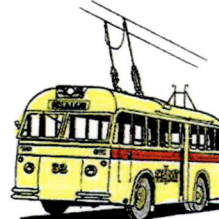

AYER ITAM
(1937)

1937 - 1956 George Town 1A, 2A GTMT/ RSJ/ GTMT R9F

1954 - 1961 George Town 2, 12, 51 - 55 Sunbeam MF2B/ BTH/ GTMT B41C
1956 - 1961 George Town 14 - 19, 25 - 34 Sunbeam MF2B/ BTH/ GTMT B41C

MAP OF GEORGE TOWN MUNICIPAL TRANSPORT
TROLLEYBUS OVERHEAD NETWORK 1924 - 1961

drawn by

Guy Arab motorbus in Penang Road heading for Green Lane.
Courtesy of F. W. York

Up till the 1950s, the tickets themselves were provided by a number of manufacturers in England. Tickets of the Bell Punch type were used and these were cancelled by the conductor tearing a piece out of them, "in" or "out" as the case may be. Oller Limited of London seems to have been the principal supplier of tickets, with sporadic supplies from the Punch and Ticket Company, also of London. Bell Punch-manufacured tickets similar to the others were also ordered from time to time.

The year 1956 saw some changes in tickets. When George Town achieved city status in that year, ticket headings were changed to suit and this provided the opportunity for a local Chinese printer, Tye Sin Press Ltd., to enter the ticket market. Tye Sin Press Ltd. produced a far superior product on very high quality paper, superior to that produced by the English counterparts, and soon became the main supplier of tickets.

Ticket machines also appeared in the form of T.I.M.M.s on an experimental basis, later being compared in use with a Mycalex machine. This meant that the ticket machine contained a blank roll and all the ticket information was printed once the conductor selected the appropriate fare and tore off the ticket for the customer; this was, in effect, a semi-automatic ticket. All ticket machines were fitted with a non-reversible recording mechanism to make tampering impossible.

Before this semi-automatic ticket was introduced, when a fare increase was found to be necessary, a modified ticket had to be improvised. For example, in order to provide a 15 cent ticket on the Botanical Gardens service, a 10 cents ticket had to be stamped with what at first appears to be a Post Office cancellation imprint, titled "Municipal Transport Services 15 cents" (note "Municipal", not "City"). The longer routes were divided into two 10 cent stages with a 20 cent through fare which, in the case of Ayer Itam at least, was still a bargain.

MOTORBUSES & EXPANSION

Meanwhile the motorbus was being returned in earnest. Of the sixteen "Military Buses", ten were kept on until 1952 in order to open a new route connecting the Jelutong terminus with the village at Pulau Tikus. Theses buses had to go before they resembled mobile scrap heaps but they managed to keep going until the arrival of four Austin buses fitted with very smart full-fronted bodies with Perkins P6 diesel engines. These proved to be economical and were given fleet Nos. 43 to 46, with two arriving in June 1952 and the other two arriving in the following autumn.

Austin motorbus No. 43 (PB 526)
which entered service in 1952,
seen at Chulia Street.
Courtesy of F.W. York

Like many other urban areas in the world during that period, a large building programme was in hand in George Town. New housing estates needed bus services, and two more Austins, Nos. 47 and 48, came into service in January 1953, but their 31-seat capacity proved inadequate and something with a bigger capacity was needed. The Guy Arab III had a heavier chassis and larger body than the Austin, and so six Guy Arab IIIs with the Gardner 5LW power plants were purchased and these, fitted with locally-built 39-seat single-deck bodywork, went into commission during April 1953. They were numbered 37 to 42, filling the gap between the highest pre-war trolleybus number and the Austins. Two more followed six months later – Nos. 49 and 50. With 14 vehicles, the bus fleet was complete for the time being and trolleybus expansion was to become the order of the day.

For a time, while some of the Ransomes were being rebodied, one or two Austins worked on the Jelutong trolleybus route and eventually a motorbus service using the outer end of the Jelutong trolleybus route and a new deviation into the town centre was regularly worked. At this time, a new trolleybus service was opened to Green Lane and Caunter Hall. Green Lane lived up to its name – tall palm trees came right up to the roadway, with the population served by the service hidden away behind a wall of green.

It should be noted that an enlightened administration issued a questionnaire in 1953 to sound public opinion on the subject of routes to be followed. Guy Arab III buses went to work on the busy Perak Road service. The popular pleasure resort, the Penang Botanic Gardens also known as Waterfall Gardens, was situated beyond the town, and until 1953 visitors had had to depend on their own motive power to get them there. At first, a limited trolleybus service was put into effect on Sundays and Bank Holidays. So successful did this route appear when initially introduced, that it was then put onto an all-day basis. However, having been thus over-serviced, it subsequently became the "Cinderella" route of the system.

In 1954 construction began on the new Transport Depot complete with offices, stores, a canteen, servicing accommodation and a covered parking space. By then the new 41-seat Sunbeam trolleybuses were in regular service. To some degree this period of recovery and development ended with the decision taken in 1954 to create a separate Transport Department distinct from the Electricity Supply Department of which it had been part. It was exactly fifty years since the electric tramway had been formed.

One disturbing problem, which first attracted attention in 1955, was the fact that fewer fares were collected than there were passengers. The passengers (it was said) too often gave their tickets back to the conductor thinking him a poor man with a family to support and so tempting him to retain the fare. The Municipal Council's annual report for that year stated the problem in plain terms:

Revenue collected from passengers was disappointing as it amounted overall to only 60.8 cents per mile. Misappropriation of fares by certain conductors had apparently increased, following the acquittal by the Court in 1954 of two conductors charged with this type of offence.

This misappropriation of fares appears to be a problem, which is nowadays frequently encountered by bus operators in Malaya excepting the many small-scale operators whose employees, and inspectors especially, are recruited mainly from the owners' relatives…

Guy Arab motorbuses and a Sunbeam MF2B trolleybus under repair at the Depot, circa 1960.

Some improvement resulted from a case in which a conductor was sentenced to six months imprisonment on two charges of criminal breach of trust. But the remedy was to replace men with women conductors. They were offered smart uniforms but firmly decided upon wearing a sort of battle-dress instead.

THE EX-LONDON TRANSPORT DOUBLE-DECKER TROLLEYBUSES

The new George Town Municipal Transport board decided, as an experiment, to purchase five ex-London Transport double-deckers in 1956. The vehicles themselves had been some of the oldest working for London Transport when withdrawn by them in 1955. These ex-C1 class AEC vehicles arrived at the Penang quayside in May and June 1956. Having already seen 20 years service they could be said to be a curious choice, but they had been well maintained by their former owners and were, even taking into account shipping charges, rather inexpensive.

Given the random order of the numbers it can be assumed that they were members of the class in best condition. In fact, while four had Metro-Cammell bodies, the fifth had a body built by Weymann.

Ex-London Transport double-deckers, newly arrived in Penang, still bearing the U.K. number plates, CGF 175 and CGF183 (above) and CGF 138 (below). They became Penang Nos. 22, 23 and 24 respectively.
Courtesy of Derek Watts

London Transport 106 (left) and London Transport 175 (right) at Bexleyheath, Southeast London; the latter was shipped to Penang where it became GTMT trolleybus No. 22 in Penang.

Courtesy of London Transport Museum

They became Nos. 20 to 24 with George Town Municipal Transport, taking the numbers formerly allocated to pre-war Ransomes trolleybuses which were withdrawn. They were numbered in chassis number order and their previous London Transport fleet numbers had been 142, 148, 175, 183 and 138 respectively. When new in London they were used on routes 657, from Isleworth Depot and 667 from Fulwell Depot, and had been replaced in 1952 by 70-seat BUT9641Ts, the last ever London Trolleybuses to be delivered – Nos.1842 to 1891. In 1952 the C1 class trolleybuses were transferred to Highgate (Holloway) depot to replace 60-seat B2 class trolleybuses and for their last three years in service had been kept to the relatively quiet "Hampstead Routes" (i.e. 513, 613, 615 and 639).

At the time many London trolleybuses were being withdrawn due to service cuts. These "lucky" five were the only pre-war trolleybuses to be sold for further use, thereby avoiding the cutter's torch for the time being.

On arrival they were towed to the depot for certain modifications. Ventilation for example was inadequate, and the solution was to fix full drop depth sliding windows. The existing seating was unsuitable as it encouraged cockroaches, so standard tropical materials were fitted. Automatic acceleration was also installed. Initially the fleet number was displayed in red on the rear registration plate and also centrally displayed on the front panel.

Trolleybus No. 23 (ex-London Transport 183) stopping in front of the police headquarters on Penang Road, on the Jelutong to Jetty service.
Courtesy of Ashley Bruce

London Transport No. 148, in London (above) and as trolleybus No. 21 in Penang (left)
Courtesy of Omnibus Society, United Kingdom and F.W.York

The London Transport C1 class trolleybus No. 142 when new (left). This vehicle was later to become GTMT No. 20 (right).
Courtesy of London Trolleybus Society, United Kingdom

Double-decker trolleybus No. 24 (ex-London Transport No.138) on the Ayer Itam route.
Courtesy of John Rossman

Staff had to be consulted as to the manning of these "giants" and conducting staff would only work on them on the principle of "one deck, one man." The Department went into consultation with the only other double-deck operator, G.T.C. of Kuala Lumpur. They used this system and found that the extra revenue earned by their double-deck vehicles more than paid for the extra man's wages. It would seem that the lower deck man held seniority and to him fell the honourable tasks of replacing poles, pulling over junction frogs and being in charge of the platform.

It is believed that these vehicles worked the Jelutong route in the beginning. The only difficulty was at the Jelutong terminus, where these longer vehicles were unable to negotiate the turning circle without reversing. Extensive road works were put in hand and the circle enlarged. In theory they could operate on all routes except the Hill Railway shuttle, and photographic evidence would suggest that fairly soon after entering service they more often than not worked the Ayer Itam route.

Initially, the double-deckers "gave a good account for themselves". The honeymoon period lasted until the novelty wore off with the travelling public. With relatively low fare levels and three crew members on board – notwithstanding the Kuala Lumpur experience – they soon became uneconomic. The double-decker buses, being cast-offs, rapidly disintegrated. Ex-Transport Department officer Tait recalled how, one day, a panel came loose to reveal the rotten pine wood inside. Thousands of cockroaches scurried out. The age of the double-deckers told against them and one can only assume that they were purchased basically to assess double-deck operation, whether for trolleybus or motorbus.

*Double-decker trolleybus
going down Weld Quay.*

*Ex-London Transport C1 class
AEC double-decker No. 23.
It was one of four purchased
that had Metro-Cammell
bodies, while the fifth was
bodied by Weymann.*
Illustration by David W.O. Jones

Double-decker No. 23 is pursued by a Guy Arab motorbus whilst working the Jelutong service.

Trolleybus No. 19, with Sunbeam MF2B chassis, only entered service in July 1956, together with Nos. 13, 14, 15, 17 and 18, replacing the older Ransomes of the same numbers.

Courtesy of Robert Sechler

Stopping at the Police HQ, Penang Road, is RSJ No. 18, one of six Ransomes replaced with Sunbeam trolleybuses in 1956.

Ric Francis collection

CITY STATUS & THE "GOLDEN SUMMER"

George Town was declared a city on 1 January 1957 and G.T.C.T., for George Town City Transport, began to replace G.T.M.T. on the sides of the vehicles. The year 1956 had seen the two small trolleybuses Nos. 1A and 2A being replaced on the Penang Hill Railway shuttle service. Two small Ransomes, rebodied No. 35 and unrebuilt No. 36, were converted to one-man operation and these became the usual replacements.

At the end of 1954 six more Sunbeam MF2B chassis had arrived and were waiting to receive bodies. The six, originally to be numbered 56 to 61 according to some sources, were expected to enter service in 1955. However, considerable delays in the completion of some electrical equipment – probably the result of earlier rail and dock strikes in the United Kingdom – caused them to be incomplete for a considerable time. The batch, which by now had been given Nos. 13, 14, 15, 17, 18 and 19 from replaced Ransomes, did not actually enter service until July 1956.

GTMT double-decker trolleybus No. 24, on the Jetty-Ayer Itam route, coming down Dato' Kramat Road, near the junction with Perak Road. The event – possibly the launch of the new bus, the celebration of city status, or Merdeka – attracted a large street crowd and was recorded by a small crew (bottom right). Note the overhead street lamp, the traffic lights with the yellow orbs and the bus stop (far left).

Right, below and facing page:
Three post-war postcards
showing Sunbeam trolleybuses at
Penang Road, passing familiar
landmarks such as Boston Cafe
and Capitol cinema. The orange
board on the trolleybus below
denotes that the vehicle is on the
Jetty-Green Lane service.
Courtesy of John Rossman

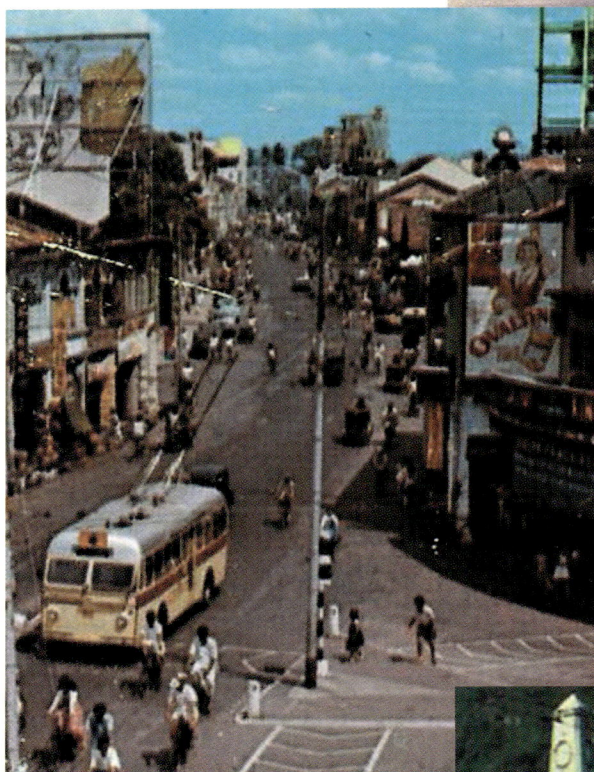

Further orders were placed for ten more Sunbeam MF2Bs to replace the last of the unmodified Ransomes and these, Nos. 25 to 34, entered service between November 1957 and March 1958. No. 33, which was the last to enter service, was to prove the last trolleybus to join the fleet.

Competition from private operators was still severe, there being three Chinese bus operators covering the trolleybus services from the town centre. One company, Lim Seng Seng Bus Co., had a sole route in common with the Ayer Itam trolleybus service. The fact that an owner of private buses was able to make a good living out of this business was a sore point to the

Replacing an old Ransomes of the
same number, this Sunbeam MF2B
entered the fleet in 1958 as bus No. 32,
only to be scrapped three years later.

Municipal operator who, rightly or wrongly, considered that this traffic should have been exclusively carried on its trolleybuses.

The services of the Council were further extended by the completion of the Penang Power Station at Udini Road, which was officially opened on 3 January 1957. The Prai Power Station ceased regular generation at this time.

At the beginning of that year the City Council had a fleet of 55 public passenger vehicles, which comprised 41 trolleybuses and 14 diesel buses. On an average day 50 were in service.

After March 1958 the trolleybus fleet had been thoroughly modernised; this was indeed the "golden summer" of George Town trolleybus operations. There were:

8 modernised and rebuilt Ransomes, Sims & Jefferies vehicles for peak and emergency use

26 modern Sunbeams

5 ex-London Transport double-deckers, plus

2 small Ransome Sims & Jefferies vehicles for the Hill railway shuttle.

Plans were drawn up for "30 modern single-deckers to be available for the basic all day services and good quality secondhand double-deck vehicles to assist with peak hour traffic."

Sample tickets used by the City Transport Department trolleybuses and buses
Courtesy of F.W. York

65

Bus No. 37 (PG8512) at the Victoria Street terminal. The Bedford SB5 was delivered in May 1967 and fitted with a Union 43 seat centre entrance body. It was typical of the George Town vehicles of the post trolleybus era.

In 1958/59, several Bedford SBO chassis were delivered and fitted with locally built bodies. One is seen here being painted and completed in the Transport Department workshop.

SWITCH TO DIESEL FLEET

When the Council came under the control of the Socialist Front, the Transport Department under Chairman Councillor Lim Kean Siew made the great mistake of deciding to change to an all diesel fleet despite having many virtually new trolleybuses. Upon implementation the Council found itself going further into the red. One reason was that electric transport was exempt from paying tax to the Road Transport Department, but with the introduction of high capacity motor vehicles, the Council found itself paying several hundred thousand dollars a year in road taxes and vastly increased maintenance costs!

Initially Bedford and then Commer supplied replacement motorbuses. Five Bedford SB1s arrived in 1959 taking the Nos. 20 to 24 from the ex-London vehicles. Over the next two years 24 Bedford SB1s were taken into stock and the final trolleybus replacements in July 1961 were six of these vehicles. The following two years saw 17 Commer Avenger CD762s taken into stock; like all motorbuses, they had locally-built single-deck bodywork, and G.T.C.T. was replaced on the sides by "Kenderaan Bandar Raya George Town". Whenever a new motorbus chassis arrived, the secretariat would call tender to local contractors to build the body. At first, the bodies were built by Seng Seng Motors, then based at Cecil Street Ghaut, but subsequently, a competitor called Union Company of Patani Road also joined the bid. Seng Seng Motors was, incidentally, better known as a manufacturer of "mosquito bus" bodies.

After the Socialist Front government took over in 1959, the Council introduced the practice of naming the buses after long-serving employees

No. 29 (PC 4125), a 1962 Commer Avenger passing the Penang Prison on route 1 from Ayer Itam to Jetty.
Colin Ganley collection

of the Transport Department. These employees were entitled to free rides on council buses. By June 1963, as many as 67 motorbuses were in stock, summarised as follows:

Type of chassis	No. in stock
Karrier FD398	1
Bedford SB1	24
Bedford SB0 P6	4
Albion Victor VT15AL	5
Guy Arab III 5LW	8
Guy Arab IV 5LW	2
Austin KP CVD P6	6
Commer Avenger TS3 CD762	17
TOTAL	67

No. 15 (PB 3883), a 1960 Bedford SB1 seen at the Jetty on route 3 to Jelutong.
Colin Ganley collection

To replace the trolleybuses on the Hill Railway shuttle a Karrier FD 398 chassis was purchased. It is seen in the process of receiving its body, built by the Transport Department. On entering service in 1960 it was given the fleet number 1.

Left: Council buses moving along Penang Road.

Bottom left: The former GTMT routes were taken over by the MPPP whose Bedford SB1 No. 5 (PB 2000) is shown here. This bus originally entered service in George Town in January 1960 as one of the "trolleybus replacement fleet".
Courtesy of Ian Lynas

Bottom right: Former GTCT / MPPP Bedford SB5 of 1974, PS 3432, still extant in a car park near Komtar, January 2005.

The former trolleybus depot at 'Tramway Road', now the MPPP bus depot with the new entrance on Lorong Kulit.
Photographs by Khoo S.N.

THE END OF TROLLEYBUSES

Once the decision was made to abandon trolleybuses in favour of motor buses, the change over was fairly swift and resulted in a real waste of useful assets. In 1959 it was decided that the double-deck experiment was not really satisfactory and that trolleybuses were uneconomic as opposed to motorbuses. This was partly due to the fact that the need for two conductors badly reduced revenue and the vehicles themselves were over 24 years old.

In November 1959, therefore, as the first stage of the trolleybus replacement programme, the ex-London Transport vehicles and the rebuilt Ransomes were taken out of service and eventually sold for scrap. By a strange coincidence, the job was placed in the hands of the 600 Group of companies, who also broke up the London trolleybuses in England. In the case of George Town, the actual company was George Cohen (Far East) Limited and it is reasonable to assume that redundant overhead and equipment may also have been dismantled by the same firm.

The old tramcar depot at Tramway Road, still standing circa 1960. Note the Sunbeam MF2B trolleybus No. 18 inside. It was later used by the Electrical Department as a work shed.
Photograph by James Tait

Shortly before the first withdrawals two late changes affected the trolleybuses. Firstly, in 1959 they were required under the new regime to carry registration plates. The ex-London vehicles therefore had Penang "PB" plates fitted to the rear where they had previously carried their London registrations. The trolleybuses were numbered *en bloc* with details set out in the fleet history listing.

Delivered in December 1958, the brand new Bedford SB0 No. 59 PA 8888 with a locally built 43 seat centre entrance body is seen here immediately prior to entering service. The bus is flanked by maintenance supervisor Chan and officer-in-charge of bus maintenance garage James Tait.

Below: Tait taking a new Bedford to the weighing station at Quarry Drive. After delivery in December 1959, this brand new Bedford SB1 PB 1558 had its 43 seat centre entrance body locally built and took the fleet number No. 22 from a recently withdrawn ex-London Transport double-deck AEC trolleybus which it was effectively bought to replace.

The 'naming the buses' ceremony held in front of the Transport Department building, erected in the mid-1950s. Before entering service, the new buses, with the employees' names which they bore, were ceremoniously unveiled by Socialist Mayor Ooi Thiam Siew in 1965. Long-serving mechanic Foo Sun Tho and chief clerk Lim Wee Bee were thus honoured.

James Tait (pictured opposite page), was a long-serving employee of the Municipal Electricity and Transport Departments. Born in 1918, he started as apprentice electrician servicing the trolleybuses in 1936. He joined the 3rd Battalion, Straits Settlements Volunteer Force, 'E' Eurasian Company. During WWII, he was called back to service the funicular railway. After the war, he was assigned to the Transport Department as officer-in-charge of the bus maintenance garage. His last position before retiring in 1975 was Workshop Superintendent of the Electricity Supply Department.

Photographs on page 70 and 71 by James Tait

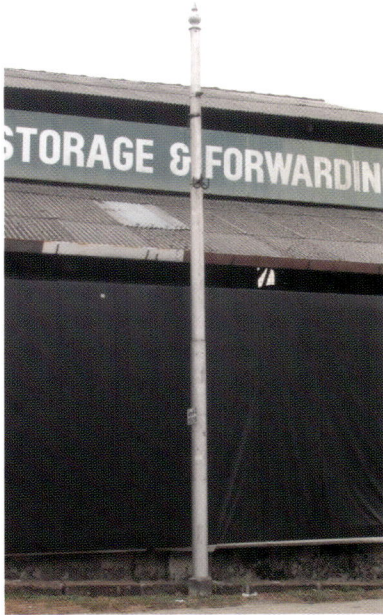

Top and bottom right: Surviving trolleybus poles at Jelutong. Right: The poles in Ayer Itam have been retained and converted to lamp posts.
Photographs by Khoo S.N.

Secondly the blinds were changed from simply showing the final destination in English to a tri-lingual English, Chinese and Malay display. Surviving routes were also latterly given route numbers; for instance Ayer Itam was route number 1 and Jelutong route number 2. When converted to motorbus the Jelutong route became route number 3.

It was decided that the Sunbeams, though far too new to scrap, were not to remain in service either. Some, in fact, barely saw three years service. Services to Ayer Itam were converted to motorbus in 1960 and redundant Sunbeams were put into store at the depot pending future sale. The Penang Hill Railway shuttle service also ceased to be trolleybus worked and Nos. 35 and 36 were withdrawn for scrap.

Twelve or thirteen vehicles lasted in service in 1961 and the day finally came when George Town lost its last electric vehicle when the trolleybuses, like the trams before them, passed into history. The last runs were made on the Jelutong route without any public ceremony, on 31 July 1961. The newest of the redundant vehicles were less than three and a half years old!

With the trolleybuses put out of service, the wiring was dismantled fairly quickly and by August 1962 the only wiring left was a few pieces of overhead in Jelutong. The traction poles were used for street lighting and many still remained at the dawn of the 21st century.

Exactly who the undertaking thought would buy the 26 Sunbeams is unclear. The nearest "neighbouring" system, Singapore, had abandoned one of its four post-war routes in December 1960 and was to close completely in December 1962, so no buyer "was on" there. *The Straits Times,* 20 December 1962, reported:

> With the complete dieselisation of its transport service the City Council is offering for sale all its 26 trolleybuses, together with 48 miles of traction wire. The sale will be by tender.

In July 1963, the Transport Manager was reported to have said that he was, *"Unable to dispose of these buses as useable vehicles."* These fine vehicles were sold for scrap, and this only emphasised the mistake George Town made in its policy of trolleybus abandonment. It certainly did not solve the financial difficulties.

Certainly the swift demise of the trolleybuses had perplexed some observers. A letter in *Buses Illustrated* No. 124, July 1965, attempted one explanation:

> The "great mystery" of the reversal of trolleybus advancement in George Town may be clarified, as from 1957 to 1959 the General Manager designate of George Town Municipal Transport was Mr. Mohamed Yunus Abu Hanifah who was undertaking professional training with Kingston-Upon-Hull Corporation Transport.
>
> The significance of this is that it was at this time that trolleybus operation was extensively studied in Hull and discussed prior to Hull's 1959 decision to replace trolleybuses by motorbuses.

Notwithstanding Yunus's presence in Hull, it has to be pointed out that the transport policy was made by the City Council, whereas Yunus was only responsible for its implementation. George Town was poorly served by this decision with its consequent profligate waste of capital assets paid for by the City. Let us not forget that motor industry interests have a long history of conspiring to supplant environmentally-friendly trolleybus electric traction in public transport with their own inferior products.

Trolleybus poles at Acheen Street and Acheen Street Ghaut — these were originally tram poles which were shortened and reused.
Photographs by Lim Gaik Siang
& Khoo S.N.

Yellow buses at the Prangin Road stand – left, the Chevrolet Maple Bus P 4845 and right, the Austin Loadstar PA 1810.
Courtesy of F.W.York

Hin Company's Morris Commercials, shadowing the blue route.
Courtesy of F.W.York

THE PRIVATE BUS COMPANIES

Three Chinese bus companies – namely, Lim Seng Seng Bus Company Limited, Hin Company Limited and Yellow Bus Service – were well-established in George Town. In the main, they duplicated the trolleybus routes within the town boundaries, although there was one exception, that being a small straightening out of the line followed towards the outer end of the Bagan Jermal service. Although there was no question of protective fares being imposed, the private buses were licensed only to a common terminal at Prangin Stand, towards the shopping centre of town and adjacent to the main markets area – well short of the all important Weld Quay and the vital connections with the ferries and the mainland.

The most peculiar bus service was that of *Lim Seng Seng* – the company's sole route was, in fact, a short working of the Ayer Itam trolleybus service, being an exact shadow all the way from Prangin Stand to the outer terminus. By coincidence, the livery of two shades of green also matched the Municipal colour identification code carried by trolleybuses, which was also green for the Ayer Itam route. Without going too deeply into the history of this situation, it is reasonable to suppose that the origins were rooted in the feeding of mosquito buses on the then

Austin K8 of Yellow Bus fleet
P 9315 on the rural route.
Courtesy of F.W.York

existing tramways. This took place during the early or middle part of the 1930s when their numbers were swelled by an influx of the little open-backed six-seaters from Singapore, following tighter regulation there to protect the new trolleybuses.

As part of a peace settlement, a controlled number of these little buses was granted licenses to continue operations. Perhaps the Licensing Authority thought that the bus company would perish once trolleybuses took over, forgetting the intense loyalty shown by the ethnic cousins of the Chinese proprietors. The colonial stratification, represented by the large proportion of expatriate officers holding senior appointments, also aroused a desire not to support the public administration (an attitude with which the Traction Company also had to contend with in Singapore). As it happened, neither operator appeared to be a threat to the other; vehicles of both operations carried good loadings, so there was sufficient business for both.

Lim Seng Seng Bus Company's
Morris Commercial, shadowing
the green route.
Courtesy of F.W.York

The majority of the Penang island population was concentrated within, or closely adjacent to, the George Town boundaries. Beyond, the villages were spread out along the coastal plain which encircled the island, the hinterland being of high hills with heavy jungle cover. Therefore, cross-island bus routes were precluded. Beyond the town,

Private buses operating from Weld Quay – the Hin Company bus (dark blue) which serviced the Weld Quay-Telok Bahang route and the Lim Seng Seng (green) bus company which serviced the Weld Quay-Ayer Itam route.

a diagram of existing bus routes would simply form a giant "C" (without being absolutely precise in navigational terms). Hin Company Limited left Prangin Stand due north-west, only to follow the western seaboard to a terminus at Telok Bahang, whilst the Yellow Bus Service travelled down the eastern coast line till past the airport at Bayan Lepas, making connections with its own mini-buses which looped around the southern tips and went up the western side up till Telok Bahang.

The *Penang Information Guide*, 1951, singled out Lim Seng Seng's bus service for praise, for offering "every comfort to passengers."

Every bus is installed with a radio receiver and the seats are upholstered with Dunlopillo cushions. The company also employs a team of young educated and polite conductresses.

The Art Deco-style Hin Company bus depot at Brick Kiln Road.

Samples of tickets used by Penang Yellow Bus Company in the 1950s.
Courtesy of F. W. York

FUNICULAR RAILWAY

View of hill railway just above the
Lower Station, with Chinese caption:
'Tramway of Penang Hill, Penang'.
Postcard courtesy of Malcolm Wade

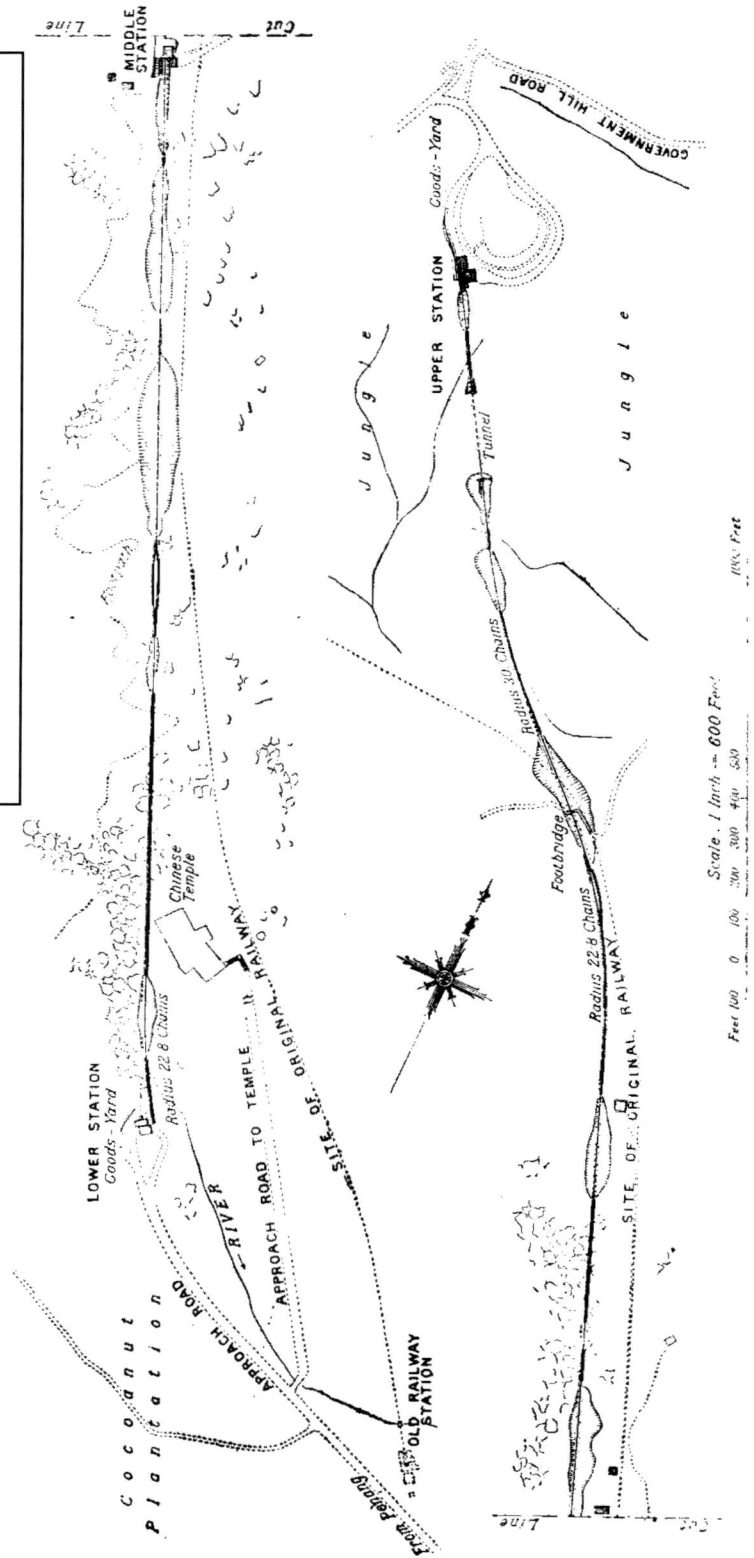

Map showing alignment of the Penang Hill Railway built in 1924. Reproduced from a paper presented by the engineer A.R. Johnson of the FMS Railways. This map also shows the 'Old Railway Station' and the 'Site of Original Railway' constructed 1898-1906.

THE FIRST HILL RAILWAY PROJECT

The two cars, No. 1 and No. 2,
that ended up as chicken houses.
Postcard courtesy of Malcolm Wade

The Penang Hill funicular railway is the only one of its kind in Southeast Asia and provides a leisurely journey through fern-covered railway cuttings, over viaducts and through a tunnel to the summit.

The first attempt at constructing a funicular railway on Penang Hill began with the formation in 1897 of a limited company called the 'Penang Hill Railway Co. Ltd.' Construction commenced in 1898 and was completed in 1906, the railway comprising only one section covering the whole distance. The motive power was a water turbine situated in a winding house at the bottom of the Hill. The design, however, was faulty and no means was ever discovered to ensure that the cars could actually move on the rails. The company accordingly went into liquidation causing the enterprise to be abandoned. The original two cars are believed to have ended up as chicken houses.

After World War I, the Straits Settlements Government desired to develop Penang Hill as an amenity in the same way as the Federated Malay States government was developing Fraser's Hill and the Cameron Highlands in central Malaya. It was decided that the Government should

Penang Hill was the earliest British hill station in Asia, offering a cool retreat from the tropical climate. It was developed as a convalescent centre, sanatorium and recreational resort for the European elite.

construct a funicular railway. This was possibly a cheaper option than building a well-graded road which, in view of the physical features of the Hill, would have had to take a long and circuitous route to the summit.

THE PRESENT FUNICULAR RAILWAY

The present hill cable railway was designed by Arnold R. Johnson, Senior District Engineer, Federated Malay States Railways, whose name had been linked with the railways as early as April 1909. Johnson was sent to Switzerland to acquaint himself with the methods of designing a funicular railway to be operated by electricity, and the Penang Hill Railway was constructed under his direction. Work began on the revamped line in 1920 and the line was opened to passenger traffic on 21 October 1923. At a ceremony officiated by the Governor of the Straits Settlements Sir Laurence Guillemard on 1 January 1924, the Penang Hill Railway was handed over by the F.M.S. Railways to the colonial government, which henceforth operated it. The line carried 35,201 passengers and made 4,021 journeys that year.

Before the funicular railway was built, European gentlemen ascended on Deli ponies while the ladies ascended by 'doolie' slung on bamboo poles and carried by four porters.

A postcard view of Ayer Itam valley, taken before 1909, probably showing the first railway cutting through Penang Hill.
Postcard courtesy of Malcolm Wade

The circa 1900 Hill Railway Station, still standing at the end of the Hill Railway Road, Ayer Itam, 2005.
Photographs by Khoo S.N.

THE PENANG HILL RAILWAY,
THE AYER ITAM TRAM & TROLLEYBUS ROUTES,
AND THE HILL RAILWAY SHUTTLE ROUTE

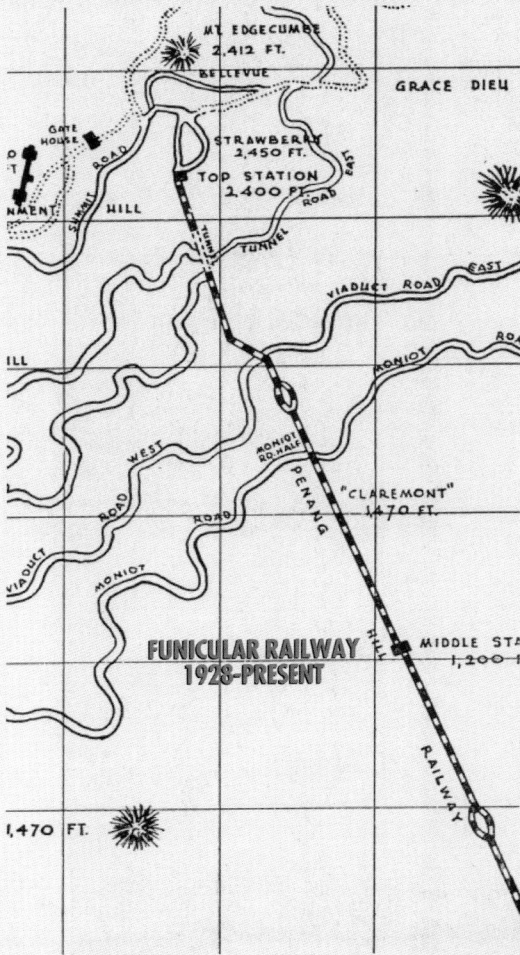

AYER ITAM-HILL RAILWAY SHUTTLE

A shuttle service ran from the junction site of the Anti-War Memorial (marked 'Chinese Memorial' on the map) to the Penang Hill Railway Lower Station. When work began on the funicular railway in 1920, a single-track branch line was initially laid to enable the Bo type locomotives to transport materials for the railway's construction. In October 1923, a public tram shuttle service was started on this line, two months ahead of the Penang Hill Railway's official opening. This was the last GTMT tram service to be switched to trolleybus operation, and in 1937 the route was taken over by two small nine-seater trolleybuses (pictured above).

PENANG HILL RAILWAY
Note how the hill roads run along the hill contours, almost perpendicular to the ascending funicular railway.

AYER ITAM TRAM ROUTE
The Ayer Itam tram route passed the Anti-War Memorial and continued to the Ayer Itam Village. Trams were replaced by trolleybuses on this route on 10 September 1936.

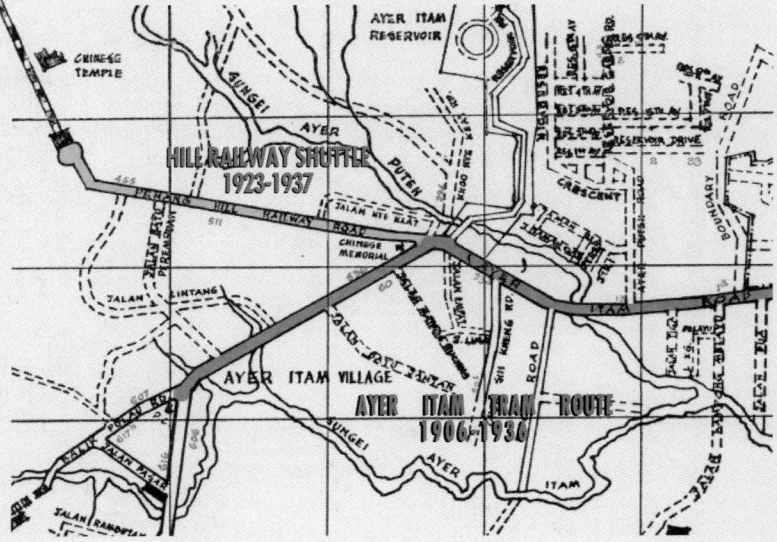

Map reproduced from 'Penang Past & Present', 1966

The funicular railway is a cable railway worked by electricity. Some interesting details of the electrical equipment of the line are contained in a paper read in 1924 before the Engineering Association of Malaya by Thomas Rogers, the deputy engineer and manager of the Electricity Supply Department, the engineer-in-chief being W.J. Williams. The following excerpts are from the paper in question:

Above: Ayer Itam-Hill Railway tram shuttle, running on a single-track branch line, arriving at the Lower Station. Below: The newly completed Lower Station of the Penang Hill Railway.

Postcards courtesy of Malcolm Wade

> The makers of the switchboard, motors and controller are British Thomson Houston Co., and the brake solenoids, Messrs. Geo. Ellison and Sons. The motor is direct-current, 75hp. fitted with interpoles.
>
> The system of supply for the railway had to be made to suit the railway specifications, which called for direct current. In order to supply this economically and fall in line with the complete electrical scheme for Penang it was decided to transmit direct current to the top of the hill at 11,000 volts and transform it in a sub station to direct current supply for the railway. This enables supply of alternating current to be available for lighting purposes on the hill without having long overhead transmission lines up the hill itself. This will also enable Prai station when finished to supply power direct to the hill sub-station.

Crossing place where the two cars pass each other.

From the Municipal sub-station, which is situated near the upper railway station, there are feeders running to both the upper and lower stations; the return wire in each case being bare copper wire which runs along the edge of each rail.

The signalling system has been supplied and designed by Messrs. Tyer and Co., and whilst somewhat complicated has given every satisfaction since being installed.

The visual signals consist of four holes in a plate, at the back of which is a second plate marked to show through the holes with the signal clear. The signal itself consists of a round red disc marked in white with the word "ready".

Signalling from the car is done by bridging with a metal fork two wires on poles running by the track. Current for lighting at night and in the tunnel is supplied by thin copper conductors mounted on ceramic insulators just outside the rails.

The tunnel is dated 1922. The stops just below and above are called Lower Tunnel Station (right) and Upper Tunnel Station (far right) respectively.

84

Note how the funicular carriage was stepped to allow for a steep incline.

The telephones on the railway may be classed as service telephones and track telephones. The service telephones are arranged to speak to one station to the other, and also from bottom station through the middle station to the top station. These are independent telephones and have no connection with either the track telephones or the Post Office lines.

TWO INDEPENDENT SECTIONS

The most famous passenger in 1972 was Queen Elizabeth II.
Photograph by James Tait

The Penang Hill Railway is built in two sections, with an interchange at the Middle Station. The passenger of the funicular railway thus gets on the train car at the Lower Station, changes trains at the Middle Station, and alights at the Upper Station.

Each section of the railway is worked independently. The car travels at 1.1 metres per second on the lower section and 1.3 metres per second on the upper section. The total length of the line along the formation level, that is, the distance between start and finish, is 1 mile 435 yards. The line rises to 2,270 feet; the mean gradient is about 1 in 3 and the maximum gradient about 1 in 1.96. The centre of the upper station is 2,381 feet above sea level. The tunnel on the upper section is 258 feet long along the formation level, and is on a gradient of 1 in 2.04. The tunnel, dated 1922, is built of granitic rock.

Perhaps the most interesting part of the train ride is the 'crossing place' at the middle of each section, where the ascending and descending cars pass each other in close proximity. Each car has two axles and the wheels on one side only are grooved so that each car can be correctly guided to follow the correct track at the passing loop.

Wayside halts are not symmetrically dispersed, as has been contrived on other similar lines. This results in the car halting "in the middle of nowhere" whilst its partner on the section calls at a stopping place. On the lower section a halt at the Chinese temple complex of Thni Kong Tnua (Jade Emperor's Pavilion), just out of the station has no corresponding halt further up.

The upper section is dotted with halts. Claremont, just under 1,500 feet up, is below the crossing point. Above that is Moniot Road, up a little further is Viaduct Station, then Lower Tunnel, whilst the Tunnel is only a couple of chains short of the upper terminus. When the car needs to stop at a halt a message is sent to the winding house to stop the cable by means of the motor man bridging the two lineside wires with his metal fork, as described earlier in the paragraph on signalling.

Automatic brakes are provided on each car to halt the car in the event of the cable breaking. The brakes are held in the "off" position by tension in the rope. When the brakes operate, brake shoes are clamped to the side of the rail on each wheel, the downward motion of the carriage being geared to supply the necessary power for clamping the rails. The brakes of each car are tested regularly to make sure the stopping distance is no more than 1 to 1.5 metres.

PRECAUTIONS IN THE WINDING HOUSE

There are four brakes in each winding house, hand brake, solenoid brake, dynamo brake and the emergency brake. The latter operates on a failure of electricity supply and arrests the movement.

The winding gear is checked daily. The winding engines are at the upper end of each section of the railway and have a "safe" pulling power of 9 tons. The winding gear is of the friction type or "Koepe" type, motive power being provided by a 75hp. electric motor directly coupled to friction pulleys through gearing. The motor is supplied with DC current by a

Passing place on upper section, August 1962.
Colin Ganley collection

The hill railway freight platform.
Ric Francis collection

100-kw rotary converter fed from the 3 phase 50 cycle 11,000-volt public electricity supply mains. Two feeders .04 sq. in., 11,000-volt three phase Callander armoured cables had been laid from the power station of the Penang Municipality to a sub-station at the top of Strawberry Hill. Here the current is transformed to 230 volts for lighting and two 300kw B.T.W. rotary converters have been installed to supply power for the railway.

The underframes of the original cars were designed and manufactured by Louis de Roll Iron Works near Olten, Switzerland, as were the automatic safety brakes, winder superstructure and cable guiding pulleys. The winding gear was manufactured by Robey & Co. Ltd. of Lincoln, England.

LOCKED COIL HAULAGE ROPES

Each haulage rope is of the full locked-coil type of construction 3.875 inches in circumference and has a breaking strength of 71.5 tons. The special steel used for its manufacture has the strength of 80/90 tons per sq. in. and the weight per yard is 11-25lbs. The strength of the rope is derived from the splicing together of lengths of wire, in the same way that hemp rope is made; as many as twenty lengths of wire are coiled around each other in an anti-clockwise direction.

The total weight of the rope is: lower section 5.5 tons, upper section 6.6 tons. Each carriage weighs 7.5 tons. With passengers another 2.5 tons is allowed. One freight wagon weighing 3.5 tons can operate with each car, with the freight wagon running uncoupled on the upper side of the passenger car.

Various patterns of freight wagon body are in use according to the type of freight carried. The wagon body is quickly detachable from the underframe and this is particularly useful for rapid transfer of loaded wagon bodies from the main line to the goods sidings at the terminal stations as well as their transfer between the two sections of the main line at the middle station. These tasks are achieved by means of gantry transporters.

The trucks carry supplies to the summit for hotels and kiosks and the railway staff quarters – tucked discreetly out of sight behind the upper station – and to schools and residences along the way. Cargoes have included a Volkswagon minibus for a hotel.

Two views of the Penang Hill Railway Middle Station.
Photograph below, Colin Ganley collection

PENANG HILL RAILWAY, NEARING TOP STATION

Above left: Ascending to the Upper Station. Above right: The hill hotel's Volkswagon minibus. Right: A Ford 'A' pick-up bus, the first passenger vehicle on the hill.
Postcards courtesy of Malcolm Wade

THE HILL RAILWAY DURING WORLD WAR II

During the early stages of the Japanese Occupation, the Upper Station was bombed. A few British soldiers had stayed behind and were being aided by the Penang Hill Railway staff. The Japanese at the Ayer Itam Police Station were tipped off. The soldiers, who were in fact hiding behind the Indian temple, got away before the bomb dropped. Unfortunately, the son of the caretaker of the Penang Hill Railway bungalow, who was looking up at the plane, was killed. The Malay stationmaster was injured.

In 1942, James Tait was pulled back into service under the Japanese administration. He was ordered to repair the railway at the Upper Station, for there was minor damage to the signal cable, telephone wire and lighting cable. As electricity supply had been disrupted, Tait had to wait for the power to resume before testing the railway operations, just in time for the visit of a Japanese VIP. Not wishing to work for the Japanese, Tait quietly slipped away and only rejoined municipal service after the war.

— Interview by Khoo Salma Nasution with James Tait, 2005

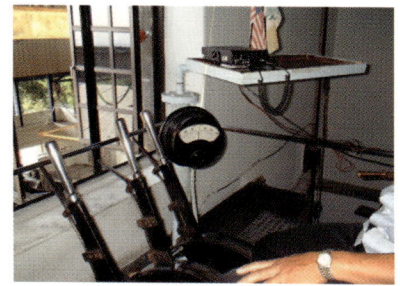

Left: The cable winding station at the top of the hill, showing the gear box for the cable winder.
Above: The cable controller.
Below: The communication phone, the cable winder and the electric motor for winder.
Photographs by Ric Francis, 2003

THE RAILWAY SERVICE

As a commercial venture the Penang Hill Railway was not an unqualified success. Its peak of popularity was in 1926 when the hill was developing rapidly. It showed a modest profit of $3,355 in 1927, but was hard hit in 1930 when building ceased. There was also a need for a hotel and restaurant at the top of the railway. By 1931 the loss on the Hill Railway amounted to £11,762.37. It was running at a loss in 1936 and showed no profit until 1937 when $1,651 was earned. It just met expenses in 1938 before plunging into new losses in 1939-40. On the credit side could be placed the hill station's usefulness to harassed officials or citizens in need of cooler air. The value of this was recognised by the Municipality when it built the "Richmond" and "South View" bungalows for its own staff, and there can be no doubt that the investment was a sound one.

There were four cars, two permanently allocated to each section, and each car capable of carrying 40 passengers, seated and standing. The maximum passenger carrying capacity of the line was about 150 passengers in each direction per hour. A two-class

Railway car ascending a viaduct; note the service steps by the side.

system operated, though the standard of comfort was the same, wooden seating. The lower end of the car was given over to first class and the upper end to second class. The obvious advantage of travelling first class, apart from it being less crowded, was the superb views to be had from the lower end of the car.

Travelling time was about 13 minutes per section. Though frequency has varied over the years, services in the early 1960s were generally half hourly, though at peak times it was possible to operate a 15-minute interval service stretching the operating efficiency to the limit. The operating day ran from approximately 06-30 to 21-00, with later cars on Wednesdays and Saturdays extending services until midnight.

Not many figures are available, but in 1960 passengers carried were 388,097 and in 1964 passengers carried had risen modestly to 391,803.

As the Hill Railway was too small an undertaking to afford its own full-time manager and engineer, the day-to-day operation, maintenance and administration were, since the completion of construction, placed under the care of the George Town City Electricity Supply Department. The railway is now owned by the Government of the State of Penang which controls all matters of policy in connection with the undertaking.

ELECTRIC RAILWAY

*The Eastern Smelting Company (ESCOY)
railway, pulled by the Bo type locomotive
No. 2, with two vertically sprung poles on
the platform, along Weld Quay.*
Courtesy of ESCOY

TIN TRANSPORT BY ELECTRIC RAILWAY

Established in 1898, the Eastern Smelting Company (ESCOY) at Dato' Kramat Road was Malaysia's largest and longest-running smelting works. ESCOY made use of the municipality's electric railway to bring stores and tin ore for its smelting works and transport tin ingots to the harbour for export.

The railway was part of the old George Town Municipal Tramways, but was latterly operated by the George Town Municipal Transport Department. The locomotives started out in life as vehicles used to transport materials for the Penang Hill Railway. The first two electric locomotives were purchased in 1920 from an American company, as were the motors. The locomotives rode on a single four-wheel truck, No. 1 having the original tramway single horizontally-sprung tramway pole centrally placed. On the closing of the tramway in 1936, a second pole was mounted behind the first so that power could be collected from the dual wires of the trolleybus system. No. 2 was originally the same but had two vertical sprung poles on the platform. Both locomotives could be run coupled together. The wheel diameter of the locomotives was 2 feet 4 inches. The motors were of the totally enclosed type with spur drive to the axles, there being one 30-hp. motor per axle. The wheel base (rail to wheel gauge) was one metre, length 11 feet and width 5 feet. Accurate figures of weight were not known but quoted at 3 tons. The control equipment was a normal tram type drum controller of B.T.H. and G.E.C. pattern.

Power was taken from the overhead system, firstly from the tramway's single overhead wire, and latterly from the trolleybus double overhead

Wagons with the initials "E.S.C. 15" bringing ore from the Eastern Smelting Company to be loaded on to the ships. At Swettenham Pier, the wagons were pulled by the Penang Harbour Board's diesel locomotives.
Postcards courtesy of Malcolm Wade

The 1893 map (modified in the early 1900s) and postcard views showing the tramline along Weld Quay and the interchange with the Penang Harbour Board's Railway at Swettenham Pier.
Map courtesy of Penang Museum

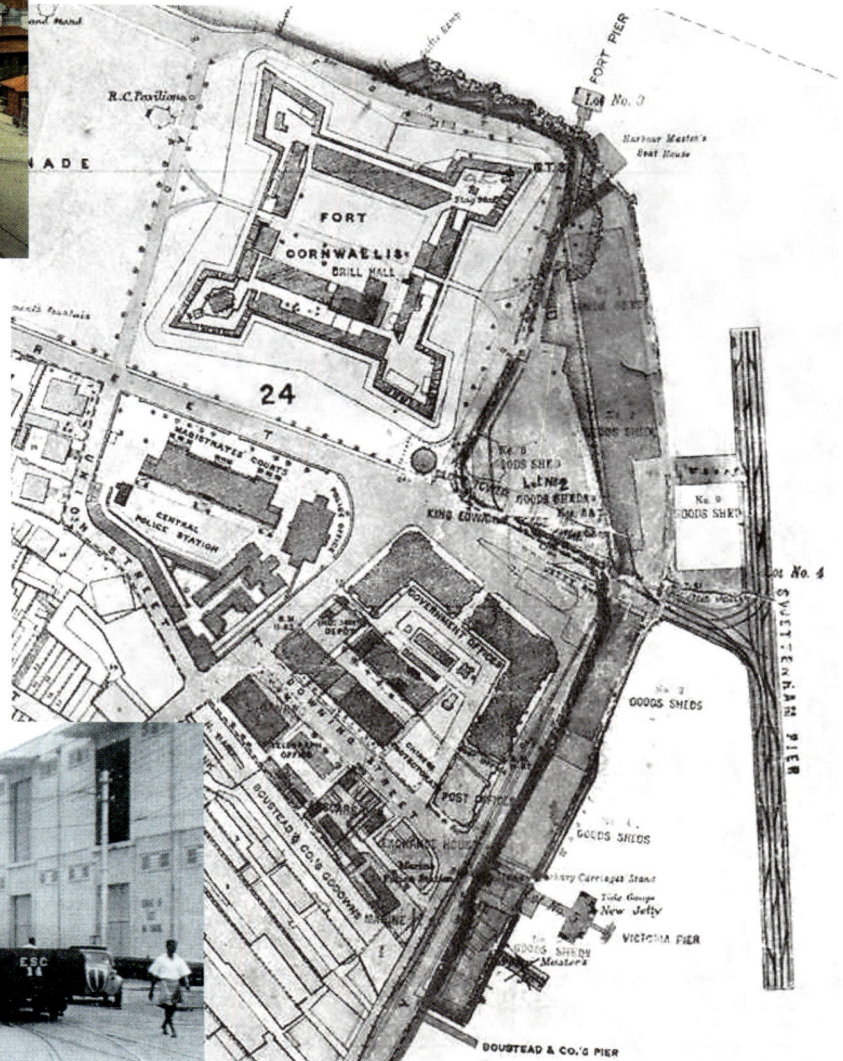

Two trains, pulled by locomotives No. 1 and No. 2 in succession, outside Swettenham Pier at Weld Quay. RSJ trolleybus No. 33 can be seen passing on the left.
Courtesy of F. W. York

*The Electric Railway sidings
extended into sheds on ESCOY
property. Here wagon No. 12 is
being loaded with ingots
which will be taken to the
godowns at the Jetty.*
Courtesy of ESCOY

wire. A third locomotive was built from scrapped tram equipment in 1936 and added to the fleet.

The electric railway system and locomotives were owned by the Municipal Tramways but the Smelting Company owned 25 wagons for transport of goods behind the locomotives. The trains ran over the old tramway line from the Penang Harbour Board property to the Eastern Smelting Works at Dato' Kramat Road, a distance of 1.7 miles. The railway was double track, metre gauge and was of normal tramway construction, being portions of the tramway route. Almost the entire track was on public roadway except for about 150 yards in the smelting works. At the other end, it joined the Penang Harbour Board's railway at Swettenham Pier – this was operated by diesel locomotives.

Loads were kept down to 25 tons per locomotive, and made up of five four-wheel five-ton open wagons. The speed limit of five mph was never exceeded and rickshaws could safely follow the trains. When using the trolleybus routes the locomotives gave way to the trolleybus and the motorman and his assistant held down the trolley-poles to allow the bus

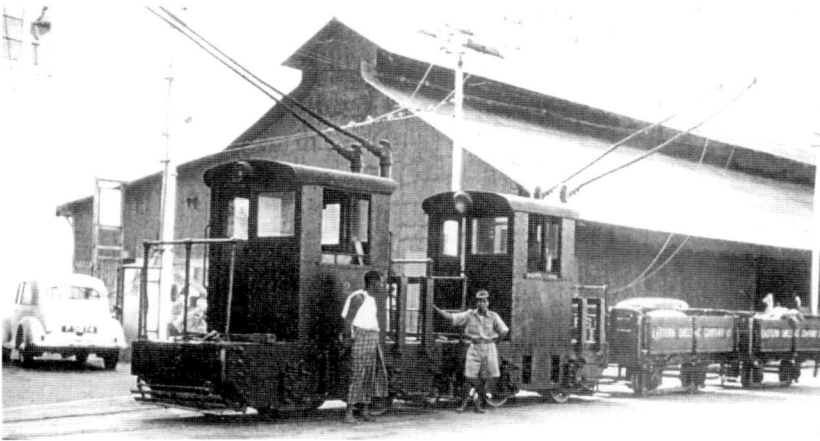

to pass. The trains intermixed with all local traffic, slowly clattering around traffic islands, and were subject to all local traffic regulations.

During World War II, the Japanese continued to use the railway for the same purpose but, to add injury to insult, they used, amongst other things, soft soap as lubrication in the axle boxes!

The track was still in good condition when motor transport took over on 1 January 1957 and the railway closed down, thus becoming part of George Town's transport history.

AERIAL TRAMWAY & SWITCHBACK RAILWAY

Right: Aerial tramway, another example of electric transport used in George Town. Here it is used by Khie Heng Bee Rice & Oil Mills to transport rice grain from the mill to the drying area across Bridge Street.
Postcard courtesy of Malcolm Wade

Below: The 1893 map (modified in the early 1900s) showing a 'switchback railway', at a site not far from the Khie Heng Bee Mills.
Map courtesy of Penang Museum

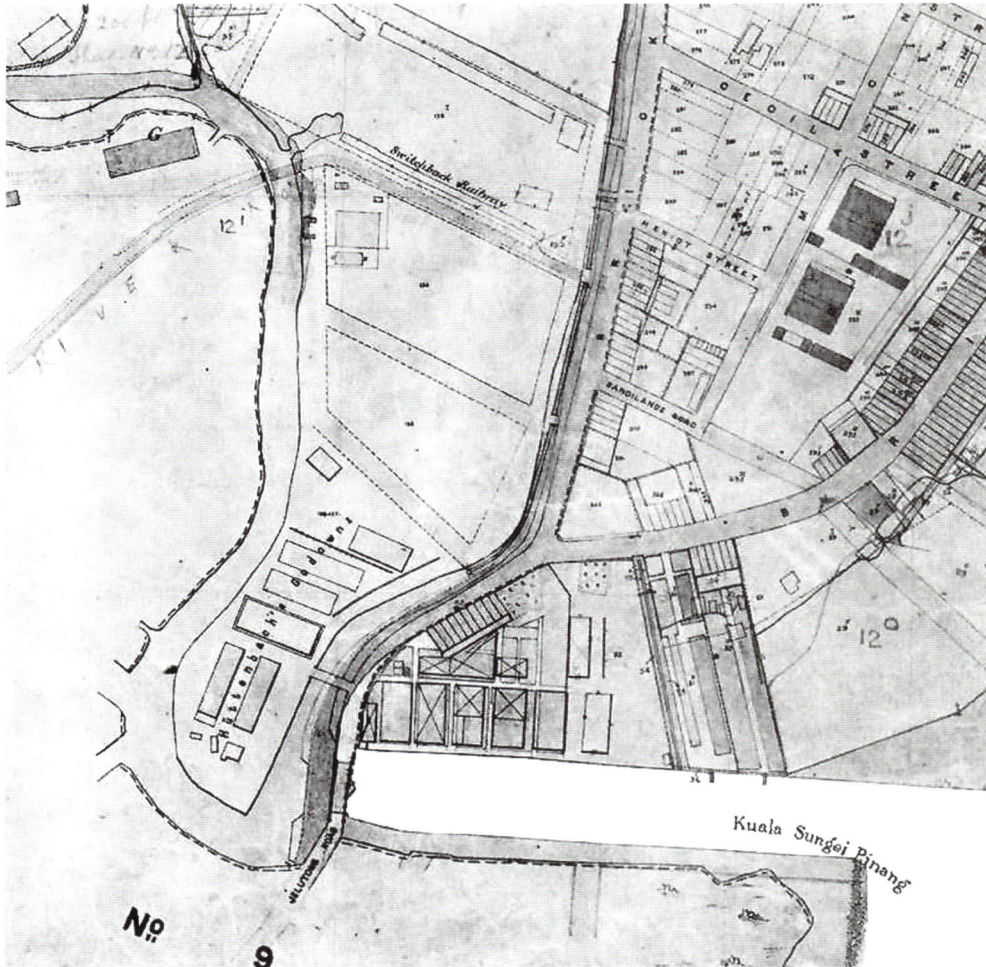

APPENDIXES

Electric tram, Ayer Itam.
Courtesy of Geoffrey Wade

PENANG HILL RAILWAY

F A R E S

(a) Ordinary Tickets:	1st Class	2nd Class
Lower to Upper/Upper to Lower Station ..	$1.60	$0.80
Lower to Middle/Middle to Lower Station ..	.80	.40
Upper to Middle/Middle to Upper Station ..	.80	.40
Lower to Thean Kong Thuah/		
Thean Kong Thuah to Lower Station ..	.30	.15
Upper to Tunnel/Tunnel to Upper Station ..	.30	.15

(b) Excursion Tickets:

(Available on Sundays & Public Holidays)

	1st Class	2nd Class
Lower Station to Upper Station (Return) ..	$2.00	$1.00
Upper Station to Lower Station (Return) ..	2.00	1.00
Lower Station to Middle Station (Return) ..	1.00	.50
Middle Station to Lower Station (Return) ..	1.00	.50
Upper Station to Middle Station (Return) ..	1.00	.50
Middle Station to Upper Station (Return) ..	1.00	.50

(c) Season Tickets.

	1-month 1st Class	1-month 2nd Class	3-months 1st Class	3-months 2nd Class
Lower to Middle Station..	$14.40	$7.20	$36.00	$18.00
Lower to Claremont Stn...	19.20	9.60	48.00	24.00
Lower to Viaduct Station..	24.00	12.00	60.00	30.00
Lower to Upper Station..	28.00	13.90	72.00	36.00

(d) Concession Tickets:

Lower to Middle Station

	1st Class	2nd Class
10 rides (3 months)	$ 5.00	$ 2.50
20 rides (6 months)	10.00	5.00

Lower to Upper Station

	1st Class	2nd Class
10 rides (3 months)	10.00	5.00
20 rides (6 months)	20.00	10.00

KERETAPI BUKIT BENDERA, PULAU PINANG.
JADUAL HARIAN
PENANG HILL RAILWAY
DAILY TIME TABLE

Keretapi Turun — Lepas daripada Perhentian Atas — DOWN TRAINS — Depart Upper Station		Keretapi Naik — Lepas daripada Perhenti an Bawah — UP TRAINS — Depart Lower Station	
6-30 (pagi) a.m.		6-45 (pagi) a.m.	
6-45 ,,		7-00 ,,	
7-00 ,,		7-30 ,,	
7-15 ,,		8-00 ,,	
7-45 ,,		8-30 ,,	
8-00 ,,		9-00 ,,	
8-15 ,,		9-30 ,,	
8-45 ,,		10-00 ,,	
9-15 ,,		10-30 ,,	
9-45 ,,		11-00 ,,	
10-15 ,,		11-30 ,,	
10-45 ,,		12-00 (petang) p.m.	
11-15 ,,		12-30 ,,	
11-45 ,,		1-00 ,,	
12-15 (petang) p.m.	(b)	1-15 ,,	
12-45 ,,		1-30 ,,	
	(b)	1-45 ,,	
1-15 ,,			
1-45 ,,		2-00 ,,	
2-15 ,,		2-30 ,,	
2-45 ,,		3-00 ,,	
3-15 ,,		3-30 ,,	
3-45 ,,		4-00 ,,	
4-15 ,,		4-30 ,,	
4-45 ,,		5-00 ,,	
5-15 ,,		5-15 ,,	
5-45 ,,		5-30 ,,	
6-15 ,,		6-00 ,,	
6-45 ,,		6-30 ,,	
7-15 ,,		7-00 ,,	
7-45 ,,		7-30 ,,	
8-15 ,,		8-00 ,,	
(a) (i) 8-45 ,,		8-30 ,,	
9-00 ,,	(a) (i)	9-00 ,,	
(a) (i) 9-15 ,,		9-15 ,,	
(a) (i) 9-45 ,,	(a) (i)	9-30 ,,	
(a) 10-15 ,,	(a) (i)	10-00 ,,	
(a) (i) 10-45 ,,	(a)	10-30 ,,	
(a) (i) 11-15 ,,	(a) (i)	11-00 ,,	
(a) 11-45 ,,	(a) (i)	11-30 ,,	
(a) (i) 12-00 Tengah Malam	(a)	12-00 Tengah Malam	
(Midnight)		(Midnight)	

(a)   Hari Rabu dan Sabtu sahaja (Wednesdays & Saturdays only)

(i)   Mungkin di-tukar dengan tiada di-beritahu (Subject to change without notice)

(b)   Hari Sabtu sahaja   (Saturdays only)

HARDIAL SINGH.
Pengurus (Manager)

GEORGE TOWN MUNICIPAL TRAMWAYS
ELECTRICAL UNDERTAKINGS
STATISTICS FOR THE PERIOD 1921 TO 1926
taken from the Guide to Electrical Undertakings, published 1927, pages 1525 and 1526
"COLONIAL – EUROPE AND ASIA"

George Town (Penang) – Tramways – Population, 134,000. Average journeys per head per annum, 54.06. The Municipal Council acquired the tramways and reconstructed lines for electric traction. Power from lighting stations at 7 cents per unit. *System* – Overhead trolley, 11.57 miles single track. Girder rails, 90lbs, and Vignoles rails in country. Rolling Stock – 21 single-deck cars and 3 trailer cars and 3 buses and 2 trolleybuses. Line opened for traffic, January 1906. *Consulting Engineers,* Preece, Cardew & Rider. *Engineer-in-Chief and Manager,* T. Rogers. *Financial Assistant,* L. M. Howlett. *Workshop Superintendent,* K. Coombs.

Capital Expenditure (1926). – $883,357.08

Units used (1921) 319,534; (1922) 340,105; (1923) 395,489: (1924) 480,906; (1925) 515,691; (1926) 599,841.

COMPARATIVE TABLE

Year ended 31st Dec.	Passenger Traffic Revenue	Operating Costs	Car Mileage	Cost of Electricity	Revenue per Car Mile	Costs per Car Mile	Passenger Carried
1921	$249,966.58	$207,850.80	463,579	$47,937.60	55.50cts	44.80cts	6,029,512
1922	$214,852.21	$181,698.10	415,523	$40,812.60	44.92 "	38.70 "	4,818,396
1923	$213,436.89	$211,637.87	615,258	$39,548.90	34.69 "	34.39 "	6,841,538
1924	$215,113.11	$196,909.18	624,564	$39,177.54	34.44 "	31.53 "	6,808,484
1925	$239,067.49	$202,797.06	663,438	$41,255.28	36.03 "	31.16 "	7,245,201
1926	$269,853.82	$248,550.93	653,888	$41,988.87	41.26 "	38.01 "	8,465,821

GEORGE TOWN TROLLEYBUS FLEET LIST 1925-1961

Vehicles shown in approximate order of delivery

Abbreviations:

GTMT - George Town Municipal Transport
LT   - London Transport
RS&J - Ransomes, Sims & Jefferies

SLT - Small Light Type
ii   - Indicated prior to the fleet number denotes second vehicle to carry this number.

Note: Withdrawal dates for pre-war RS&J vehicles are based on when the vehicle was replaced by a post-war replacement. All Sunbeam types were stored on withdrawal following route closures and were all still extant at the depot in 1963, their dates of withdrawal being when most likely they were last used in traffic.

Date in Service	Fleet No.	Chassis and Chassis No. (if known)	Body	Withdrawn
1925 (new 03/24)	1	Clough-Smith No.14	Brush B30D (Orig. 6 1st cl, 24 2nd cl)	1952
1925 (new 05/24)	2	Thornycroft No. 9839X	Strachan & Brown B28D (Orig. 6 1st cl, 22 2nd cl)	10/52
1927	3	RS&J C-type	RS&J/GTMT B35R Rebodied to GTMT B24C 1954/5	1959
1927	4	RS&J C-type	RS&J/GTMT B35R Rebodied to GTMT B24C 1954/5	1959
1927	5	RS&J C-type	RS&J/GTMT B35R Rebodied to GTMT B24C 1954/5	1959
03/29	6	RS&J C-type	RS&J/GTMT B35R – later B35C Rebodied to GTMT B24C 1954/5	1959
03/29	7	RS&J C-type	RS&J/GTMT B35R Rebodied to GTMT B24C 1954/5	1959
03/29	8	RS&J C-type	RS&J/GTMT B35R Rebodied to GTMT B24C 1954/5	1959
03/29	9	RS&J C-type	RS&J/GTMT B35R Rebodied to GTMT B24C 1954/5	1959
03/29	10	RS&J C-type	RS&J/GTMT B35R – later B35C Rebodied to GTMT B24C 1954/5	1959
12/29	11	Modified Thornycroft motorbus chassis No. 1143? rebuilt by GTMT	GTMT B26C	3/53
11/31	12	Modified Thornycroft motorbus chassis No. 1145? rebuilt by GTMT	GTMT B26C	3/53
05/35	13	RS&J SLT, No. 2434	GTMT B24R	1956
05/35	14	RS&J SLT, No. 2435	GTMT B24R	1956
02/36	15	RS&J SLT	GTMT B26C	1956

Date in Service	Fleet No.	Chassis and Chassis No. (if known)	Body	Withdrawn
02/36	16	RS&J SLT	GTMT B26C	Destroyed in WWII
11/36	17	RS&J SLT	GTMT B26C	1956
11/36	18	RS&J SLT	GTMT B26C	1956
11/36	19	RS&J SLT	GTMT B26C	1956
11/36	20	RS&J SLT	GTMT B26C	1956
11/36	21	RS&J SLT	GTMT B26C	1956
11/36	22	RS&J SLT	GTMT B26C	1956
11/36	23	RS&J SLT	GTMT B26C	1956
11/36	24	RS&J SLT	GTMT B26C	1956
11/36	25	RS&J SLT	GTMT B26C	1957
11/36	26	RS&J SLT	GTMT B26C	1957
11/36	27	RS&J SLT	GTMT B26C	1957
11/36	28	RS&J SLT	GTMT B26C	1957
11/36	29	RS&J SLT	GTMT B26C	1958
11/36	30	RS&J SLT	GTMT B26C	1950
07/37 (built 1935/6)	1A	GTMT using parts from RS&J battery refuse truck and Morris 30cwt chassis	GTMT B9C One-Man-Operated	1956
07/37 (built 1935/6)	2A	GTMT using parts from RS&J battery refuse truck and Morris 30cwt chassis	GTMT B9C One-Man-Operated	1956
08/38	31	RS&J SLT	GTMT B26C	1958
08/38	32	RS&J SLT	GTMT B26C	1958
01/39	33	RS&J SLT	GTMT B26C	1958
01/39	34	RS&J SLT	GTMT B26C	1958
04/40	35	RS&J SLT	GTMT B26C Original body destroyed in WWII Rebodied to GTMT B36C in 1951 Latterly One-Man-Operated	1960
04/40	36	RS&J SLT	GTMT B26C Latterly One-Man-Operated	1960
02/53	ii 1	Sunbeam F4 No. 50742	GTMT B24C	1960
02/53	ii 16	Sunbeam F4 No. 50743	GTMT B24C	1960
02/53	ii 11	Sunbeam F4 No. 50744	GTMT B24C	1960
10/54	ii 2	Sunbeam MF2B No. 80073	GTMT B41C	1960
10/54	ii 12	Sunbeam MF2B No. 80072	GTMT B41C	1960

Date in Service	Fleet No.	Chassis and Chassis No. (if known)	Body	Withdrawn
10/54	51	Sunbeam MF2B No. 80075	GTMT B41C	1960
10/54	52	Sunbeam MF2B No. 80071	GTMT B41C	1960
10/54	53	Sunbeam MF2B No. 80069	GTMT B41C	1960
11/54	54	Sunbeam MF2B No. 80074	GTMT B41C	1960
11/54	55	Sunbeam MF2B No. 80070	GTMT B41C	1960
07/56	ii 13	Sunbeam MF2B No. 80094	GTMT B41C	1960
07/56	ii 14	Sunbeam MF2B No. 80092	GTMT B41C	1960
07/56	ii 15	Sunbeam MF2B No. 80095	GTMT B41C	1960
07/56	ii 17	Sunbeam MF2B No. 80093	GTMT B41C	1961
07/56	ii 18	Sunbeam MF2B No. 80096	GTMT B41C	1961
07/56	ii 19	Sunbeam MF2B No. 80091	GTMT B41C	1961
06/56	ii 20	AEC 664T No. 664T013	M.C.C.W. H40/30R (ex-LT No. 142 built 10/35 – withdrawn by LT 06/55)	13/11/59
06/56	ii 21	AEC 664T No. 664T015	M.C.C.W. H40/30R (ex-LT No. 148 built 10/35 – withdrawn by LT 03/55)	13/11/59
05/56	ii 22	AEC 664T No. 664T042)	M.C.C.W. H40/30R (ex-LT No. 175 built 10/35 – withdrawn by LT 06/55)	13/11/59
06/56	ii 23	AEC 664T No. 664T057	M.C.C.W. H40/30R (ex-LT No. 183 built 10/35 – withdrawn by LT 06/55)	13/11/59
06/56	ii 24	AEC 664T No. 664T059	Weymann H40/30R (ex-LT No. 138 built 10/35 – withdrawn by LT 03/55)	13/11/59
11/57	ii 25	Sunbeam MF2B No. 80123	GTMT B41C	1961
11/57	ii 26	Sunbeam MF2B No. 80121	GTMT B41C	1961
12/57	ii 27	Sunbeam MF2B No. 80122	GTMT B41C	1961
12/57	ii 28	Sunbeam MF2B No. 80125	GTMT B41C	1961
01/58	ii 29	Sunbeam MF2B No. 80124	GTMT B41C	1961
01/58	ii 30	Sunbeam MF2B No. 80128	GTMT B41C	1961
01/58	ii 34	Sunbeam MF2B No. 80126	GTMT B41C	1961
02/58	ii 31	Sunbeam MF2B No. 80130	GTMT B41C	1961
02/58	ii 32	Sunbeam MF2B No. 80129	GTMT B41C	1961
03/58	ii 33	Sunbeam MF2B No. 80127	GTMT B41C	1961

TOTAL NUMBER OF TROLLEYBUSES IN SERVICE (YEAR END) 1925-1961

YEAR END (No. in stock)	Clough-Smith	Thornycroft	RS&J C-type	RS&J C-type rebodied rebuilt	GTMT Thornycroft	RS&J SLT	RS&J SLT rebodied	GTMT RS&J/ Morris 9-seater	Sunbeam F4	Sunbeam MF2B	Ex-LT AEC 664T D/D
1925 (2)	1	1									
1926 (2)	1	1									
1927 (5)	1	1	3								
1928 (5)	1	1	3								
1929 (11)	1	1	8		1						
1930 (11)	1	1	8		1						
1931 (12)	1	1	8		2						
1932 (12)	1	1	8		2						
1933 (12)	1	1	8		2						
1934 (12)	1	1	8		2						
1935 (14)	1	1	8		2	2					
1936 (30)	1	1	8		2	18					
1937 (32)	1	1	8		2	18		2			
1938 (34)	1	1	8		2	20		2			
1939 (36)	1	1	8		2	22		2			
1940 (38)	1	1	8		2	24		2			
1941 (38)	1	1	8		2	24		2			
1942 (38)	1	1	8		2	24		2			
1943 (37)	1	1	8		2	23		2			
1944 (36)	1	1	8		2	22		2			
1945 (36)	1	1	8		2	22		2			
1946 (36)	1	1	8		2	22		2			
1947 (36)	1	1	8		2	22		2			
1948 (36)	1	1	8		2	22		2			
1949 (36)	1	1	8		2	22		2			
1950 (36)	1	1	8		2	22	¬	2			
1951 (36)	1	1	8		2	21	1	2			
1952 (34)			8		2	21	1	2			
1953 (35)			8			21	1	2	3		
1954 (42)			8	¬		21	1	2	3	7	
1955 (42)				8		21	1	2	3	7	
1956 (40)				8		10	1		3	13	5
1957 (40)				8		6	1		3	17	5
1958 (41)				8		1	1		3	23	5
1959 (28)						1	1		3	23	
1960 (13)										13	
1961 (nil)											

GEORGE TOWN MOTORBUS FLEET
(KENDERAAN BANDAR RAYA GEORGE TOWN), JUNE 1963

FLEET SUMMARY

Type of chassis	No. in stock
Karrier FD 398	1
Bedford SB1	24
Bedford SB0 P6	4
Albion Victor VT15AL	5
Guy Arab 111 5LW	8
Guy Arab IV 5LW	2
Austin KP CVD P6	6
Commer Avenger TS3 CD762	17
TOTAL	**67**

All vehicles were fitted with a locally-built single-deck body

KNOWN FLEET DETAILS

Fleet No. & Reg. No.		Chassis and Chassis No.		Date in Service	Body
1	?	Karrier FD 398	?	05/60	B16F
2	PC 1201	Bedford SB1	86899	08/61	B43C
3	PB 1818	Bedford SB1	71742	01/60	B43C
4	PB 1991	Bedford SB1	73333	01/60	B43C
5	PB 2000	Bedford SB1	71766	01/60	B43C
6	PB 2020	Bedford SB1	71757	01/60	B43C
7	PB 2022	Bedford SB1	73181	01/60	B43C
8	PB 2233	Bedford SB1	73092	01/60	B43C
9	PB 2244	Bedford SB1	74372	01/60	B43C
10	PB 3636	Bedford SB1	77285	05/60	B43C
11	PB 3663	Bedford SB1	77457	05/60	B43C
12	PB 3737	Bedford SB1	77437	05/60	B43C
13	PB 3773	Bedford SB1	77279	07/60	B43C
14	PB 3838	Bedford SB1	77053	07/60	B43C
15	PB 3883	Bedford SB1	77061	07/60	B43C
16	PC 1202	Bedford SB1	86900	09/61	B43C
17	PC 1203	Bedford SB1	87292	09/61	B43C
18	PC 1204	Bedford SB1	86885	09/61	B43C
19	PC 1205	Bedford SB1	88026	09/61	B43C
20	PB 1111	Bedford SB1	70829	11/59	B43C
21	PB 1515	Bedford SB1	71842	11/59	B43C
22	PB 1558	Bedford SB1	71847	12/59	B43C
23	PB 1559	Bedford SB1	71752	12/59	B43C
24	PB 1771	Bedford SB1	70839	01/60	B43C
25	PC 1206	Bedford SB1	88027	09/61	B43C
26	PC 1207	Commer Avenger TS3 CD762	0182	09/61	B40D

KNOWN FLEET DETAILS (CONTINUED)

Fleet No. & Reg. No.		Chassis and Chassis No.		Date in Service	Body
27	PC 1208	Commer Avenger TS3 CD762	0148	09/61	B40D
28	PC 4124	Commer Avenger TS3 CD762	0185	02/62	B40D
29	PC 4125	Commer Avenger TS3 CD762	1719	02/62	B40D
30	PC 4126	Commer Avenger TS3 CD762	1718	01/62	B40D
31	PC 4127	Commer Avenger TS3 CD762	1717	02/62	B40D
32	PC 4767	Albion Victor VT15AL	79152C	04/62	B40D
33	PC 4768	Albion Victor VT15AL	79143C	04/62	B40D
34	PC 4769	Albion Victor VT15AL	79148B	03/62	B40D
35	PC 4770	Albion Victor VT15AL	79142L	03/62	B40D
36	PC 4771	Albion Victor VT15AL	79143A	04/62	B40D
37	PA 1004	Guy Arab III 5LW	FD71575	04/53	B39C
38	PA 1005	Guy Arab III 5LW	FD71576	04/53	B39C
39	PA 1006	Guy Arab III 5LW	FD71577	04/53	B39C
40	PA 1007	Guy Arab III 5LW	FD71578	04/53	B39C
41	PA 1008	Guy Arab III 5LW	FD71579	04/53	B39C
42	PA 1009	Guy Arab III 5LW	FD71580	04/53	B39C
43	PA 526	Austin KP CVD P6	184047	06/52	B31C
44	PA 527	Austin KP CVD P6	184053	06/52	B31C
45	PA 528	Austin KP CVD P6	188330	10/52	B31C
46	PA 529	Austin KP CVD P6	188332	11/52	B31C
47	PA 923	Austin KP CVD P6	188329	01/53	B31C
48	PA 924	Austin KP CVD P6	188331	01/53	B31C
49	PA 1628	Guy Arab III 5LW	FD71826	09/53	B39C
50	PA 1629	Guy Arab III/5LW	FD71825	09/53	B39C
51	PC 6278	Commer Avenger TS3 CD762	2909	06/62	B40D
52	PC 6279	Commer Avenger TS3 CD762	2937	07/62	B49D
53	PC 6280	Commer Avenger TS3 CD762	2939	06/62	B40D
54	PC 6281	Commer Avenger TS3 CD762	2938	07/62	B49D
55	PC 6282	Commer Avenger TS3 CD762	2940	07/62	B49D
56	PA 6928	Guy Arab IV 5LW	FD73732	11/57	B39C
57	PA 6929	Guy Arab IV 5LW	FD73738	11/57	B39C
58	PA 8887	Bedford SB0 P6	61757	12/58	B43C
59	PA 8888	Bedford SB0 P6	61747	12/58	B43C
60	PA 9622	Bedford SB0 P6	64336	04/59	B43C
61	PA 9623	Bedford SB0 P6	64324	04/59	B43C
62	PC 5879	Commer Avenger TS3 CD762	2911	05/62	B40D
63	PC 5880	Commer Avenger TS3 CD762	2908	05/62	B40D
64	PD 2621	Commer Avenger TS3 CD762	00916	05/63	B49D
65	PD 2622	Commer Avenger TS3 CD762	00917	05/63	B49D
66	PD 2623	Commer Avenger TS3 CD762	00915	05/63	B49D
67	PD 2624	Commer Avenger TS3 CD762	00914	05/63	B49D

NOTE: Details are taken from various sources, none of which record the exact registration number nor chassis number for No.1. Most details are from records kept by Majlis Perbandaran Pulau Pinang (MPPP) from 1979. This source makes no reference to No.1 which would appear to have been erroneously omitted. Dates of entry into service are all from the 1979 MPPP records and may differ slightly from those reported in various articles in "Buses Illustrated". Differences are usually at the most by one or two months.

The electric tram on Weld Quay, circa 1910

BIBLIOGRAPHY

BOOKS

Bishop, R. A., *The Electric Trolley Bus*. London: Sir Isaac Pitman & Sons Ltd., 1931.

Johnson, Arnold Robert, *Selected Engineering Papers: No. 26 The Penang Hills Railway*. London: The Institution of Civil Engineers, 1925.

Khoo Salma Nasution & Malcolm Wade, *Penang Postcard Collection 1899-1930s*. Penang: Janus Print & Resources, 2003.

London's Trolleybuses: A Fleet History. London: The PSV Circle and The Omnibus Society, 1969.

Lumb, Geof, *British Trolleybuses 1911–1972*. Shepperton, Middlesex: Ian Allan, 1995.

Penang: Past & Present, 1786-1963: A Historical Account of the City of George Town since 1786. Penang: The City Council of George Town, 1966.

Penang Information Guide 1951. Penang: K.H. Khaw (publisher), 1951.

York, F.W., *Bus Journeys Through Malaya in the 1950s*. Croydon: DTS publishing, 2001.

Wright, Arnold and H.A. Cartwright, *Twentieth Century Impressions of British Malaya: Its History, People, Commerce, Industries, and Resources*. London: Lloyd's Greater Britain Publishing Company, Ltd., 1908.

MAP

George Town, Pinang, Surveyed by H.L. Pemberton, 1893, F.W. Kelly, Superintendent of Survey, 1893. Courtesy of the Penang Museum. [The base map dates from 1893, but it includes modifications from the early 1910s.]

ARTICLES

Bus & Coach, August 1938.

York, F.W., 'A short history of Georgetown City Transport', *Buses Illustrated* 73 & 74, April/May 1961.

York, F.W., 'Georgetown developments', *Buses Illustrated* 92, October 1962.

Porter, A.F., 'Four tickets to Kuching', *Buses Illustrated* 113 & 115 August/October 1964.

York, F.W., 'Malaysian-Notebook: The Georgetown trolleybuses', *Buses Illustrated* 121, April 1965.

Buses Illustrated 124, July 1965.

Bonford, P., 'An Electric Railway in Malaya', *The Electric Railway & Tramway Journal*, 1938.

'The Penang Hill Railway', *The Electric Railway and Tramway Journal*, June 13, 1924.

Archer, P.A., 'Far-Eastern Funicular', *The Railway Magazine*, August 1974.

The Straits Times, December 20, 1963.

The Tramway and Railway World, April 14, 1927.

The Tramway and Railway World, November 20, 1924.

'A third repeat order from Penang: Ransomes Electric Trolleybuses' [Advert], *The Tramway and Railway World*, May 15, 1930.

'Lightweight Trolleybuses for Penang', *The Transport World*, March 14, 1935.

'Georgetown Municipal Tramways', *The Transport World*, September 10, 1936.

'Penang standardises on Ransomes Trolleybuses' [Advert], *The Transport World*, June 16, 1938.

INDEX

ABOUT THE AUTHORS

Ric Francis started his career at Western Australian Government Tramways in Tramway Engineering. He then joined the Australian Army as a member of the Royal Australian Electrical & Mechanical Engineers for 12 years.

He was co-founder of the Perth Electric Tramways and supervised the laying of the Perway & Overhead line wiring of the system. He is currently a member of Electric Trolleybus Group.

He has just completed a book entitled 'Kalgoorlie Transport History 1901-2001 (Goldenlines).' Currently, he aims to research and record the histories of tramways in Asia.

Ric Francis was Lions International District Chairman 201W1 once and twice President of Lions Club of Stirling of which he has been a member for 30 years. He was awarded the World President's Award for his leadership.

Colin Ganley presently lives in Oswestry, United Kingdom, with his wife Susan and grown-up daughter Alex. He works as a Registration Executive for the UK Land Registry in Telford.

A lifelong bus and rail enthusiast, he is a member of several British train and bus preservation societies and has had several articles published in British national and transport society magazines. Colin has a vast collection of pictures and coloured slides, many of which came from his late friend, the transport historian John Strange. His extensive collection of books and bus, trolleybus and tram models and an OO scale model railway occupy a whole large room in his house.

Colin's interest in George Town's transport stems from the period 1960 to 1963, when his father worked for the British Government in Singapore. Visiting Penang during school holidays, he developed a keen interest in the local transport systems, particularly the trolleybuses of George Town and Singapore. Desiring to find out more about the George Town trolleybus system, he contacted Ric in 2000 at the start of the project from which this book evolved.

RSJ Type 'C' trolleybus approaching King Edward Place
on the one-way Jetty terminal loop.
Courtesy of Geoffrey Wade